*The Dialogues*

Also by Luciano De Crescenzo
in Picador

Thus Spake Bellavista
The History of Greek Philosophy
  Volumes I and II

*Luciano De Crescenzo*

# *The Dialogues*

translated from the Italian by
Avril Bardoni

published by Pan Books

First published under the title *Oi Dialogoi* 1985 by
Arnoldo Mondadori Editore S.p.A., Milan

First published as a Picador hardback in Great Britain 1991 by
Pan Books Ltd, Cavaye Place, London SW10 9PG

9 8 7 6 5 4 3 2 1

© Arnoldo Mondadori Editore S.p.A. 1985

This translation © Avril Bardoni 1991

ISBN 0 330 31654 0

Photoset by Parker Typesetting Service, Leicester

Printed in England by Clays Ltd, St Ives plc

This book is sold subject to the condition that it
shall not, by way of trade or otherwise, be lent, re-sold,
hired out, or otherwise circulated without the publisher's prior
consent in any form of binding or cover other than that in which
it is published and without a similar condition including this
condition being imposed on the subsequent purchaser.

The value of a dialogue depends largely upon the diversity of the views expressed. Had the Tower of Babel not existed, we should have had to invent it.

Karl R. Popper

## Contents

Foreword   ix
Papa's Mancini   1
On the Stroke of Midnight   31
Socrates and the Bumper Question   46
San Gennaro's Last Miracle   62
The Day Before   83
Socrates and the UFOs   109
The Double   115
The Landlord's Lament   136
Socrates and Television   153

# Foreword

I dedicate these *Dialogues* to my parents.

My father's name was Eugenio De Crescenzo. He was born in 1879 and fought in Albania during the First World War as a corporal. The only military feat of his that I know about (and he told the story over and over again) was to survive on army rations with mouse-shit. When I was a boy, every time I left something on my plate he would immediately start bawling: '*Io m'aggio magnate 'e cacate 'e zoccola in Albania e chistu vezziuso adda lassà tutta sta grazzia 'e 'Ddio!*'[1] The good food I was leaving was, I hasten to add, the fat I painstakingly cut away from the meat at Sunday lunch.

As a lad, my father had wanted to be a painter like his father before him. Giuseppe De Crescenzo had been a pupil of De Nittis and rather less than a leading light in the Resina school. Nevertheless, it was Grandfather who managed to nip that particular whim in the bud. Catching his son playing truant from school one day in the Galleria with a box of paints tucked under his arm, he laid about him with such gusto that they both ended up in police custody. Grandfather was required to promise that he would refrain from beating up his son and my father, in exchange, had to promise to abandon his palette for good. '*Si te vuò muri 'e famme 'e 'a fà 'o pittore!*'[2] This, in a nutshell, was Grandfather's attitude to his own profession. The very next day my father was removed from his grammar school and sent to work as a labourer in the glove factory belonging to a relative,

---

1 'I ate mouse-shit in Albania yet here's this spoilt brat wasting good food!'
2 'If you want to starve, be a painter!'

Cavaliere Martusciello. There was no Workers' Act in force in those days, so my grandfather, despite the family connection with the boss, had to pay two lire out of his own pocket to buy my father a pair of glove-maker's shears. It was, however, only a loan. At the end of the first week he, not his son, collected the pay-packet.

In time, my father rose to the position of departmental head and eventually decided to set up in business for himself, with a shop in Via Chiaia and some assistants in the workshop behind it. The business was not the immediate success that he had anticipated, though. He paid his way but somehow it never took off. My mother always laid the blame entirely on light-fingered workmen and the salesgirls who, she said, filched the merchandise as soon as his back was turned. As soon as she took over the running of the shop, things changed dramatically. In the first place, they moved to Piazza dei Martiri, a chic location much frequented by English tourists, then they fired all the workers and the salesgirls and engaged new ones, and finally my mother, managing, like St Anthony, to be in two places at the same time, kept an eagle eye on the workshop, the salesgirls and even on my father who was in the habit of presenting at least one pair of gloves to anyone who came into the shop and claimed to be a painter.

Every now and then father would say: 'I wish I had a million!' He never achieved his ambition, one reason being that during the famous raid on 4 August 1943, at precisely one-thirty in the afternoon, the shop in Piazza dei Martiri received a direct hit from an American bomb which effectively curtailed any commercial activity. He was lucky to lose only the shop and not his life, given that a few months previously he had decided to move to a more peaceful location, far from the perils of war, a place where, he proudly announced, even newspapers were unknown. That place was Cassino.

My mother, Giulia Panetta, was born in 1883 in Via Mancini in the Duchesca. At forty she was still a spinster. Neighbours were saying, *'Puverella, nunn' 'a avuta ciorta!'*[3] And yet, long after she

---

3 'Poor girl, she's had no luck at all!'

herself had become resigned to the prospect of dying an old maid, lo and behold a man, middle-aged and intent on matrimony, appeared on the horizon, a man with a business, white hair, blue eyes and a 'good name'. Family spies reported: 'He's such a nice man, not a debt to his name!' They married and went to live in Santa Lucia.

When I was born, my father was fifty and my mother forty-five. This very large difference of age between myself and my parents meant that neither of them survived to witness the development of my career. Papa died during my first year at University and Mama when I was still working for IBM. I don't know if Paradise exists or not, or if either of them made the grade, but I certainly hope so. Where my mother is concerned, I have no doubts at all: if there is a Paradise, she is there. One could even say that she had a legitimate claim. Home, work and church, church, work and home: my mother spent her whole life working and praying. I am rather less certain about my father because of his habit of railing against the Almighty in moments of stress. Though, thinking about it, he never really blasphemed. No sooner were the words '*Mannaggia a* . . .'[4] out of his mouth than my mother would interpose a 'Blessed be his name', rendering the profanity inaudible.

Paradise probably does exist. The reason we have no first-hand information is that the inhabitants have no way of communicating with us and know nothing of what is happening on earth. So isolated are they that every time there's a new intake of souls, Papa and Mama are probably there, at the gates of Paradise, questioning all the newly arrived Neapolitans.

'Where are you from?'

'Naples.'

'Which part?'

'Vomero.'

'Do you know anything about a certain Luciano De Crescenzo?'

'Who, the writer?'

'No, my son is an engineer,' my mother would reply with

[4] A malediction.

some pride in her voice. 'He works for Upim.'[5]

I worked for IBM for nearly twenty years, but my mother, for reasons unknown, never came to grips with the name of the company which she invariably confused with Upim.

'There's actually a Luciano De Crescenzo, an engineer, who does television programmes about computers,' the new arrival would say, 'but it's the same chap I was talking about, the writer. He's got grey hair and a beard. Has your son got a beard?'

'Certainly not!' my mother would exclaim. 'They would never have allowed him to grow a beard at Upim. And anyway, my son is shy, not at all the type of person to be a television presenter. He's such a quiet boy!'

'Forgive my persistence,' the shade continues, 'but your son is not, by any chance, the producer of the film *Thus Spake Bellavista*? The reason I ask is that I enjoyed that film enormously. I saw it three times!'

'No, that's not my son. You must be talking about someone completely different.'

Then one fine day (or not so fine, depending on one's point of view), I too would arrive in Paradise.

Imagine the reunion: hugs and kisses, my mother in tears, my father and I asking a hundred and one questions at the same time, trying, in fact, to compress a whole life into a few minutes.

'How are you?'

'Well enough, considering that I've just died.'

'So what have you been doing all these years? Tell us all about it! No need to hurry, though, you can take your time. After all, one thing we're not short of here is time.'

So I would tell them everything that had happened since their death: my work as an engineer, computers, resigning from IBM, the first books, the television programmes, the volume of photographs of Naples, the history of Greek philosophy, the films, the move to Rome, et cetera, et cetera.

'Just a moment, there's something I've been meaning to ask you,' my father would interrupt. 'Didn't you use to say you

---

5 A chain of departmental stores.

wanted to go in for hydraulic engineering? Yet you landed up in computers!'

'Yes. I chose hydraulic engineering because I'd heard about the dreadful condition of Italy's waterworks. There were dams to be built, embankments to be repaired, we suffered from flooding, crumbling earthworks, landslides and communities without proper drainage. In fact, I believed at the time that hydraulic engineers were indispensable ...'

'But?'

'But the only regular employment I could get was in computers.'

'Then what happened?'

'After I was made a manager there came a point when I got fed up with office routine and gave in my notice.'

'*Gesù, Gesù,*' I can hear my mother saying, 'you might have ended up on the streets!'

'So I decided to become a writer.'

'So that gentleman we spoke to a year ago was right after all. Giulia, do you remember the man from Milan who arrived with all his family after a car crash on the autostrada?'

'Of course I do! He said, "Signora, I assure you that your son is a writer." And I said, "He can't be, you must be joking," and he said, "I'm hardly likely to be in the mood for joking after what's happened to me!"'

'But how much do writers earn?'

'Well, if one's lucky enough to hit on a bestseller, a real blockbuster that stays at the top of the lists for a good long time, one can earn a tidy bit.'

I would be about to tell him, but my mother would advise me to keep my voice down.

'Sh ... *nun te fà senti*.[6] There's a lot of jealousy around here.'

'But aren't we in Paradise?'

'Yes, but one shouldn't let other people hear one's private affairs,' my mother would say with a glance over her shoulder.

'So, with the books on Greek philosophy, which have been

---

6 Don't let them hear you.

translated into several languages including Japanese, I earned something like...'

Following my mother's advice and speaking in a whisper, I would mention the total earnings from the books.

'Millions?!!!' my father would gasp incredulously.

'Of course, millions,' I would repeat.

'So you're a millionaire?'

'Papa, nearly everyone in Italy's a millionaire now!'

'*Gesù, Gesù, cos'e pazze!*[7] Gloves must be selling like hot cakes!'

'In point of fact, not many gloves are being sold at all.'

'How come?'

'People just don't wear gloves any more.'

'You know what that means, Giulia?' my father would remark to my mother. 'They may be millionaires, but elegance has gone by the board. I always said that style is a matter of breeding. A man can get rich overnight, but if he hasn't got class he'll always look like a tramp.'

'Talking of which, Papa, you haven't by any chance met a man up here called Socrates?'

'A man with a positively disgusting lack of taste in his clothes, short and plump with a face like a bulldog?'

'That's the one.'

'He's always around, but if you want my advice, steer clear. He's the sort of chap who never lets go once he's got hold of you. You've only got to say, "You're quite right, Socrates," for him to reply at once, "So, by telling me that I'm right, you are stating that you see the reason behind my argument. Then tell me, if you would be so kind, what is reason?" My son, if you want a peaceful eternity, there are four or five people to whom you should give a wide berth: Socrates, Cicero, Silvio Pellico and Cambronne.'

7 Jesus! That's incredible!

*The Dialogues*

# Papa's Mancini

'The highest concentration of artists the world has ever seen occurred in Greece between 460 and 430 BC during the famous Golden Age of Pericles...'

'Achilles' friend?' asked Salvatore, thinking it was time he made a contribution to the discussion.

'I'm afraid not,' sighed Bellavista resignedly. 'That was Patroclus. Salvatò, you haven't been paying attention for some time now, and today you've been up and down like a yo-yo, first to get a coffee, then to investigate a noise in the courtyard, and now, to cap it all, you confuse Pericles with Patroclus, leap-frogging a mere trifle of six centuries!'

'I'm sorry, Professò,' replied Salvatore contritely, 'but I keep thinking about that story you were telling us yesterday. Do you remember? The one about Achilles crying over Patroclus. I mean, I find it odd that a macho type like Achilles could get so worked up about a transvestite.'

'Whatever gave you the idea that Patroclus was a transvestite?'

'You did, Professò. From the way you told the story, I gathered that there was "something going on", as they say, between Achilles and Patroclus.'

'Listen, Salvatò. Apart from the fact that homosexuality was commonplace in ancient Greece, Achilles and Patroclus were simply two friends who spent a lot of time together, rather like you and Saverio.'

'Wait a moment, Professò,' said Saverio hastily, 'Salvatore and I are good friends, certainly; I wouldn't dream of denying it; but before you compare us to those two, let's get one thing clear. The relationship between Achilles and Patroclus has always been slightly ... dubious, one might say, so if you insist on comparing us, at least be kind enough to liken me to Achilles and Salvatore to Patroclus.'

'What do you mean by likening you to Achilles and me to Patroclus?' asked Salvatore suspiciously.

'I know what I mean,' replied Saverio.

'Look here,' interrupted Professor Bellavista impatiently, 'if you don't mind, I should like to get on with the lesson. If you have other ideas tell me now and we'll declare the session closed.'

'No, Professò, for heaven's sake please continue!' exclaimed Colonel Santanna before turning to the twin sources of the disturbance and adding, in a rather different tone of voice: 'It's too bad, *site sempe vuie dduie ca facite ammuina!*'[1]

'So, as I was saying,' Bellavista continued, 'the fifth century BC was a period of outstanding artistic activity in Greece. The salons of Athens were thronged with painters, sculptors, architects, philosophers and the writers of plays and comedies.'

'Why were there so many of them all at once?' Salvatore asked, by way of atoning for his previous lack of attention.

'No one knows. One of Nature's mysteries,' the Professor replied. 'Some historians believe that the catalyst responsible for this sudden blossoming of the arts was Pericles himself, the ruler of Athens...'

'Catalyst?' Saverio echoed in the vain hope that Bellavista might be moved to explain the term.

'Others, however,' the Professor continued regardless, 'attribute the phenomenon to the character of the Athenian people. Imagine, the people were so fond of contests and gambling that they organized competitions for everything under the sun: they would pit two painters, two singers, even two orators at times, against each other just to see who was the best.'

'Just like tennis matches, more or less,' remarked Saverio.

'Talking about tennis, I can't stand McEnroe,' murmured Salvatore, wrinkling his nose. 'I saw him on television yesterday,

[1] 'It's always you two who create mayhem!'

and he struck me as being a nasty piece of work and very bad mannered.'

Everyone turned towards Salvatore, signalling reproof for this latest irrelevant interjection.

'There was one contest between two painters, Zeuxis and Parrhasius, which went down in history,' Bellavista continued, having quelled Salvatore with a withering look. 'A wooden stage had been erected specially for the occasion in the middle of the agora so that everyone could be involved in judging the paintings. According to the rules of the contest, both paintings had to be covered with scarlet cloths until the last moment, when they could be unveiled one at a time. The one that then received the most applause would be accounted the winner. By drawing lots, it was decided that Zeuxis' work was to be seen first. The painting showed a bunch of grapes. Now, believe it or not, the painting was so realistic that birds flew down to perch on the picture and peck at the grapes.'

'Good God!' exclaimed the Colonel.

'At which Zeuxis, now confident of winning, turned to his opponent and said: "Sorry about this, Parrhasius, but I think you've lost the contest. Still, lift up the curtain and let's see what you've done." "I can't," replied Parrhasius. "The 'curtain' is only painted!"'

'That,' declared Salvatore, 'is what I call art! Not like all this modern rubbish!'

'Talking about modern art,' said Luigino, 'a cousin of mine who's a shop steward at Enel[2] told me they've planned a works outing for next Sunday. They're all going to an Exhibition of Modern Art at the Villa Pignatelli. He said that there are still three or four places free and there'd be no problem if we wanted to go along, provided we didn't make ourselves too conspicuous. He said they're even organizing lunch-boxes.'

'What's a lunch-box?' asked Salvatore.

'A picnic meal,' replied Luigino.

'And what will that consist of?' enquired Salvatore.

2 The National Electricity Board.

'Salvatò, what a lot of questions you do ask!' protested Luigino. 'It's all free. They'll take you by coach to the Villa Pignatelli, show you the exhibition of Modern Art, feed you – and as if that wasn't enough, you ask what's in the lunch-box! Tell me something: if the menu is not to your liking, what will you do? Stay at home?'

'No, I might come even so,' Salvatore replied phlegmatically. 'But since I know already that I don't like modern art, I just hoped I might at least enjoy the lunch-box.'

'Professò,' said Saverio, 'tell us the truth. You really prefer nineteenth-century painting, don't you?'

'Well, let's put it this way. I grew up surrounded by little oil paintings of Neapolitan seascapes. My father was a great admirer of the Posillipo school. Every so often he came home with what he called an "absolute bargain". For a few days he refused to show it to anyone for fear that my mother would accuse him of throwing money down the drain, then he would show it just to us children. He would place the picture on a small easel at the far end of the room with a light shining on it, and we had to go in with our eyes closed. When he said "open your eyes" we would see him smiling at us as if to say, "See what a bargain I've got this time!"'

'Incidentally, Professò,' said Salvatore, 'when I was down in Mergellina yesterday, at the beach chalets, I heard about a family trying to sell a Mancini to raise some cash.'

'Antonio Mancini?'

'That I don't know, but they said it's a lovely picture. There's one snag, though, because while the head of the family, a certain Bonajuto, wants to sell, his wife objects because, she says, the painting's a memento of her father.'

'So?'

'So if you want it you'll have to go when the wife's not at home. I'll find out more if you want me to.'

Filiberto Bonajuto, an expert in heraldry and a fencing-master, was fond of describing himself as 'one of those people who missed the train in the nineteenth century and found themselves by default in the twentieth, the age of the computer.' His favourite imprecation was: 'Devil take electricity and whoever invented it! Where do you think the Rolling Stones would be today without electricity? Nowhere, nowhere at all!'

Bonajuto ('mind, we spell it with a j') was an accepted authority in his own field. In his hands the most ordinary surname, Esposito[3] excepted, revealed aristocratic blood. In less than a month he could trace a family tree back seven generations and guarantee, at the very least, a connection with the cadet branch of an aristocratic but impoverished family. Gaudioso became, after intensive research, Claudioso, and was then transformed into Claudius to reveal, eventually, undoubted descent from the Claudian family and the Emperor Tiberius himself; this was all set out on a parchment certificate, countersigned by a retired notary, illustrated with a coat of arms and handed over with the warm congratulations of Filiberto Bonajuto. But despite this, things never went really well and every now and then he would have to sell off something from the house, a carpet, say, or a picture. Today it was the turn of the Mancini.

'What have I got to offer by way of skills? I'm a fencing-master. Do you, my dear Professor, happen to know anyone who needs a fencing-master to arrange a duel? No? Of course not. The fashion today is all for muggings, contract killings, gunning people down with automatics. And here I have to admit my ignorance. I don't know how to fire a Kalashnikov. I could teach etiquette ... let's see ... the art of kissing hands ... the principles of Jacopo Gelli's Code of Chivalry, perhaps? But who to? Signora Ammaturo who runs the electrical shop in the Duchesca, or her daughter who goes off to meet her punk friends in the disco every night? No. I'm sorry, but I'd rather stay out of it. Never mind, I was born into the wrong century and must put up with the consequences.'

Bellavista listened to the heraldry expert unburdening himself

---

3 Esposito was the name given to foundlings accepted by the religious houses in Naples, and is therefore extremely common. *Translator's Note.*

and waited impatiently for the moment when he would decide to reveal the famous Mancini painting. There, in the dining room, it was not in evidence. The walls were only adorned with two yellowing prints of no value and an even more depressing calendar with a view of Venice.

'So, are you going to show me the Antonio Mancini?' he said at last, rather aggressively.

'Immediately,' replied the old gentleman, rising. 'If you would be kind enough to come this way...'

Opening the door to the sitting room, Bonajuto went in and stopped dead. The room was in darkness apart from a small light illuminating a picture on the far wall.

'There it is. Antonio Mancini, *The Nurse*. Oil on canvas, signed and dated 1883, when the artist was still a patient in the mental hospital. The woman in the picture was his nurse.'

Filiberto turned on the central light and took the picture down from the wall so that Bellavista could examine it more closely.

The Professor, to make no bones about it, had always longed to own an Antonio Mancini but market prices had always, alas, placed it beyond his reach.

'It's probably way beyond my resources,' said Bellavista, 'but it costs nothing to ask the price. How much would you take?'

'Professò, I must be straight with you, because the sooner we know where we stand, the better. This is an authentic Mancini, given by Antonio Mancini himself to my father-in-law when he visited him in hospital. It also has considerable sentimental value for the family, but that is not your concern...'

'I realize that. But if the price is too high...'

'Luckily for you,' continued Bonajuto, 'it's only an oil sketch, probably not quite complete, so the price is reasonable: two million and it's yours. Of course, had it been finished and with every last touch put in, I should not have let it go for less than a hundred million; but unless I am much mistaken, you are not the sort of man to be put off by such trifles. It is no less a Mancini for being unfinished, and remains the work of a genius whose output was possibly at its finest precisely during those years of mental illness.'

'I suspected it would be too expensive for me,' sighed Bellavista, genuinely disappointed. 'I'm afraid I shall have to deny myself. The fact is that, Mancini or no Mancini, I cannot afford to splash out more than a million on a painting.'

'A million?' echoed Bonajuto, crestfallen. 'To be honest, that is not enough and would not even enable me to settle my most pressing debts. And you cannot imagine the domestic ructions I shall have to cope with if I sell this Mancini! They would make your hair stand on end. My wife has always been against it. I can hear her now: "The Mancini is a memento of my father. We'll sell anything you like, but not Papa's Mancini." But by gentle persuasion, day after day, I have nearly brought her round. This evening, when the poor woman comes home and sees that light patch on the wall . . . Professò!'

Bellavista, intent on the painting, was not listening.

'Professò,' Bonajuto repeated, striving to catch his attention, 'can you see that light patch on the wall? Believe me, there'll be some heartache this evening!'

At last Bellavista raised his eyes from the painting and looked at the patch on the wall. Much as he desired the painting, he could not help feeling twinges of remorse at the thought of Signora Bonajuto's distress.

'Which reminds, me, Professò,' the fencing-master continued, 'if we want to get everything settled, we should do so now, before my wife returns. Maria will be home at any moment and I don't want her disturbing us while we're talking business.'

'Look,' said Bellavista apologetically, 'I'm not for one moment questioning the sentimental value this painting has for you and your wife. But that doesn't alter the fact that my own circumstances at this moment are such that I cannot spend more than I have already offered you. At the very most I might go to one million two hundred thousand.'

'But Professò, one million two hundred is really not realistic!' protested Bonajuto. 'We're talking about a Mancini! Do me a favour, if you will, and examine the portrait more closely. Look at this, can you not see the demented mind behind this brushstroke?'

'Where?'

'Here, Professò. Look at the white apron. This is no mere handiwork, this is a sabre-stroke of white lead, the colour hurled in fury at the canvas! My dear Professor, you are looking at madness made visible in paint, the cry for help from a prisoner who longs for freedom. Imagine a volcano one minute before an eruption and you will have some idea of what Mancini must have been like on that day.'

'Look,' murmured Bellavista, on the point of surrender, 'let's say one million three hundred and there's an end to the matter. Summer's on its way and I've got holidays to think about...'

The Professor was still trying to justify his latest offer when a woman entered the room behind him, a middle-aged lady rather shabbily dressed in a dark-grey coat, an emaciated fox-fur round her neck and a black leather handbag clutched in her hands. She paused in the doorway, her eyes brimming with tears, watching the two men silently for a few moments before saying, very quietly:

'Filiberto, you're selling Papa's Mancini!'

'No,' replied Filiberto, 'I was just showing it to this gentleman.'

'Liar!' retorted Signora Maria, her voice much shriller than before. 'You're selling Papa's Mancini!'

'I was trying to come to an arrangement.'

At these words, Signora Bonajuto suddenly threw down her handbag, leaped at her husband and tried to snatch the picture out of his hands.

'You bastard! You're not going to sell the Mancini! If you sell the Mancini, it will be over my dead body!'

Bonajuto moved even faster. Quick as lightning, he passed the picture to Bellavista and immobilized his wife by pushing her against the wall and holding her there with all his strength. Then he cried:

'Professò, leave a cheque for one and a half million on the table and take the picture... but be quick... leave the house, I can't hold her back much longer... Take the picture...'

\*

'And here we have an example of the work of one of the major exponents of Modern Art, Alberto Burri.'

Professor Salemi, expert on contemporary painting and now acting as guide for the party from Enel, paused a couple of metres away from a picture consisting of a canvas to which a sack with a dozen or so patches in it had been glued.

'For the benefit of anyone who doesn't already know,' Salemi continued, 'Alberto Burri, together with Ballocco, Capograssi and Colla, initiated the first authentic school of non-representational painting in Italy...'

'Excuse me, Professor,' asked a member of the group, 'but what is the painting called?'

'*The Big Sack*. A work of the Fifties,' replied Salemi without hesitation.

Finding the title appropriate enough, everyone nodded with satisfaction, some even screwing up their eyes the better to appreciate the significance of the work. Salemi, meanwhile, proceeded with his exposition.

'How can we understand Burri? Well, gentlemen, I should like each one of you to concentrate on the painting until you can feel, in the depths of your own being, the pain the artist was trying to express. Observe, if you will, the gaping holes in the cloth, the wounds encrusted with bitumen, the white of the quick-lime, the rending of inert matter, and perhaps you will succeed in penetrating the essence of a work which has rightly been described by the critics as "an inconography of suffering".'

Everyone tried to concentrate, each according to his own capacity. Saverio and Luigino also gazed at the work, striving in all good faith to understand it, until Saverio noticed out of the corner of his eye that Salvatore was about to put a question to their illustrious guide.

'Hey! What are you up to?'

'Nothing,' replied Salvatore, 'I only wanted to ask the Professor something.'

'You just keep your mouth shut!' retorted Saverio sternly. 'We can talk later, when we're on our own.'

The shop steward who arranged their inclusion in the party

had solemnly warned the three not to bring themselves to the notice of any works official. He had said, 'Listen, chaps, do me a favour, no comments and above all no larking around'.

'And after Burri, here is Fontana!' announced Salemi, and stopped in his tracks as if struck by lightning. Fontana was evidently one of his favourite artists.

The party grouped itself as best it could around the work and for a few seconds no one dared to breathe. The work in question was a beige-coloured canvas in the centre of which the artist had executed, probably with a razor blade, a diagonal cut. Saverio, Salvatore and Luigino looked at the cut in silence and exchanged private glances.

'When one is discussing Fontana,' Salemi began, 'it is inappropriate to speak of painting. Indeed, let's be precise and admit, once for all, that in the works of this master there is no true distinction to be made between painting, sculpture and the graphic arts in the sense in which these terms have traditionally been applied to the different *genres*. Fontana himself, in his *Manifesto Blanco*, has specifically repudiated any classification.'

Salvatore could restrain himself no longer. He was on the point of opening his mouth when Professor Salemi turned and spoke directly to him: 'Now, you might well want to put the question: "So if it is not a picture, what is it?"'

'Exactly, Professò; you took the words right out of my mouth!' exclaimed Salvatore, happy at this invitation to speak. 'What is it?'

'It is a Spatial Concept.'

'Is that the title?'

'No, the title is *Expectation*.'

'And this one?' asked Salvatore, pointing to the next picture, where there were five cuts.

'*Expectations*.'

'Plural!'

'Yes, and that again is a Spatial Concept,' stated Salemi.

'Professò,' enquired Salvatore, 'was that all Fontana ever did, make cuts?'

'No,' replied Salemi, 'there is also a series of holes.'

'Just cuts and holes, then,' Salvatore concluded.

'Can't you get it into your head to keep your mouth shut!' muttered Saverio into his ear, gripping his arm and holding him back as the rest of the party moved on.

'What are you on about!' protested Salvatore. 'The Professor asked me a question and I answered him!'

Meanwhile, the others had moved through to the next room. Luigino walked beside the guide while Saverio and Salvatore stayed at the back, arguing.

'If you go on like this, you'll get all three of us slung out, and if that happens we won't even get our lunch-boxes!' said Saverio. 'Don't you realize that we're gatecrashing?'

'But sometimes the words just come out by themselves.'

'You've got to stop them coming out! Don't you think that I feel the same? *Io stò comme a 'nu passo!*[4] retorted Saverio. 'But as you see, I don't speak. I give my stomach a pinch and keep my mouth shut!'

'I'll tell you one thing, and that's that my legs are beginning to ache,' grumbled Salvatore, 'and I can't understand why they don't have more chairs around in these museums so that people can sit down when they want to rest.'

'Don't worry,' said Saverio consolingly, 'there's only one more room to do and then we're going to have lunch.'

Before he had finished speaking, Luigino came hurrying back with his eyes popping.

'Hey, you two, you'll never guess what's in the next room. A toilet!'

Salvatore and Saverio, their curiosity aroused, hurried off and had barely entered the adjoining room before seeing, affixed to the wall on their right, a complete bathroom. No detail had been omitted. There was a bathtub, a pale blue mat, tiles on the wall, a pedal bin, and even a yellow handtowel.

'Tom Wesselman: *Bathtub, collage No. 8*,' Salemi announced with a note of pride in his voice. 'Wesselman is a prominent exponent of American Pop Art. By juxtaposing three-dimensional

---

4 It's driving me mad!

painting and objects of everyday use, the painter's intention was to mount a satirical attack against mass hedonism. The technique employed is that of "mixed media", by which we mean a composition that is part painting, part collage of objects that...'

Salemi's voice tailed off as he became aware of an altercation behind him. Everyone turned round to see Salvatore sitting on an old chair and being verbally attacked by one of the Villa Pignatelli staff.

'Will you or won't you get up from that chair!'

'I'll get up in a minute,' replied Salvatore. 'The fact is that my legs are really a bit tired.'

'Then go and sit down on the benches in the foyer. You can't sit here: this is a picture.'

'What do you mean, a picture?'

'I mean just that, a picture!' replied the custodian, more heatedly than ever. 'Can't you see that this chair is chained to that picture behind it? If you don't believe me, read what's written here.'

Still seated, Salvatore turned to read the label on the wall:

'Robert Rauschenberg: *Pilgrim*, 1960. So what?'

'So now you get out of the chair!' yelled the custodian. 'I've had nothing but problems with these chairs! It's incredible how every single person has to sit down as soon as they get to this point!'

'Then why don't you do something about it,' said Salvatore helpfully. 'Put a notice on it, saying: ATTENTION. THIS IS NOT A CHAIR, IT'S A PICTURE!'

Let's get this straight, Salvatò,' said Saverio. 'You don't know anything because you left school at eleven; I don't know much more because I left at fourteen, but these people have all got degrees in art appreciation ... they read *Repubblica* ... How can you expect two ignorant devils like us to understand more than these learned people who, besides everything else, are rich and have money to spend? What I say is this, that if so many educated people say that modern art is important, it means there's got to be something in it and that these painters really are artists.'

'So what you're saying is that if I'd had more schooling I'd have liked the picture with the chair.'

'Of course you would,' said Saverio forcefully, 'because you would have got the message.'

'The message of the chair?'

'Exactly.'

'Maybe in that case,' conceded Salvatore, 'I might have liked the picture with the sack. But even if I studied for the rest of my life I don't think I'd ever like the one with the chair.'

'What do you know about art!' exclaimed Saverio. 'As I said, it's all a matter of getting things straight. It's impossible that for the past eighty years, ever since modern art began, no one should have noticed that it was all rubbish! So let's accept the evidence and admit that it is us who don't understand it.'

The conversation was taking place at the home of Bellavista. Salvatore, Saverio and Luigino had been giving a detailed account of their visit to the Exhibition of Modern Art.

'It's a shame you weren't there, Professò,' said Salvatore. 'You'd have enjoyed it, honestly. As far as I'm concerned, I thought this exhibition of Modern Art was much better than the seventeenth-century one we saw last year at Capodimonte. There were too many saints in that one, too many religious pictures, it was like being in a church! This one was jollier, livelier.'

'Don't mind him, Professò,' Saverio interrupted. 'Salvatore didn't understand a thing. And he kept trying to interrupt the guide, an important professor, just taking the mickey out of him. If I hadn't stopped him . . .'

'But I wasn't taking the mickey out of anyone, Professò!' protested Salvatore, pained. 'I was trying to understand, that's all. Anyway, I'm very curious to know what you think about modern art.'

'That's a tough one,' said Bellavista after a pause for reflection. 'Perhaps tougher than it seems. Art, as I see it, is one of the ways in which men communicate with each other. Painters, sculptors, musicians and – why not – writers too, all try to communicate an idea or an emotion through their art to those at the other end, the consumers as they say on the television. Now I would say that every time they succeed in communicating an emotion, that is Art; if the recipient feels nothing, it is not Art.'

'So you're saying,' Salvatore objected, 'that because I didn't feel anything when I was looking at that picture with the slash across it, the one by . . .'

'Fontana,' prompted Saverio.

'Fontana,' echoed Salvatore, 'it means that there was no communication and the picture wasn't Art?'

'Precisely,' said the Professor. 'Without a doubt Lucio Fontana is not Art where Salvatore's concerned, but he could be Art for Bellavista.'

'I don't understand. Is it Art or not Art?'

'Salvatò, there was a Greek philosopher who denied the existence of Truth . . . Truth in the sense of something absolute, something that's the same for everyone. This was Protagoras of Abdera. Protagoras said: "Man is the measure of all things, of things that are that they are, and of things that are not that they are not".'

'And what did he mean by that?' asked Salvatore.

'You see, you don't understand the message!' exclaimed Saverio. 'And that's because you haven't studied books.'

'Protagoras was saying,' explained Bellavista, 'that we are each the centre of the universe. Everyone has to decide what is and what is not. If all you see in Fontana is a vandal who slashes pictures to make a fool of his fellow man, Protagoras won't tell you you're wrong. He'd say: "Salvatò, Fontana is not Art". But he'd agree with me as well, because every time I look at a work by Fontana I have a strange feeling, like the feeling a bird must have when it's flying between the earth and the moon.'

'No, Professò,' Salvatore protested, standing up. 'You're just playing with words and trying to pull the wool over my eyes. You can't feel anything of the sort. I'd bet that everyone who was at that exhibition yesterday felt exactly the same as me, only they didn't have the guts to admit it. Even Saverio, who doesn't know his arse from his elbow and wouldn't spend a fiver on a picture, was just being a smarmy hypocrite when he said to the professor who was showing us around: "Fontana's certainly a very striking painter!"'

'So what,' said Saverio defensively. 'I only said it to make him happy. I saw that he had a certain weakness for that particular artist and I wanted to, how shall I put it . . .'

'Humour him,' suggested Bellavista.

'Exactly, I wanted to humour him. And there's something else I want to say, too. Just imagine the hell this Fontana must have gone through.'

'In what way?' asked Salvatore.

'It's obvious. Think how he must have been teased by his pals when he was young and before he became famous.' Here Saverio started to act the part of Fontana's hypothetical friend: '"Lucio, what have you been doing today? Working on another picture? You must be worn out!" Shrieks of laughter. And he must have had problems with his cleaning lady too. I can just imagine him saying to her: "Caterì, when you're doing my studio, mind you never throw anything away. Even if you find a canvas full of holes, don't chuck it in the bin: it's worth millions!"'

'In fact, Professò,' added Salvatore, 'all these modern painters must have a hard time before they get known. But what I find puzzling is how posterity will deal with them.'

'Posterity?' enquired Saverio.

'Yes, posterity, the people who'll be around in the year three thousand. I'll give you an example. I once read a report in *Il Mattino*[5] about someone finding a picture by Raphael under the rubble of an old villa. The builder who discovered it netted a fortune. Now, let's suppose that in the year three thousand, under the rubble of the Villa Pignatelli, someone finds a work by Wasserman . . .'

'Wesselman,' Bellavista corrected him.

'OK, Wesselman . . . that one with the bathtub I was telling

---

5 The daily paper of Naples.

you about. What would our builder of the thirtieth century make of that? Would he say he'd discovered a work by Wesselman or that he'd found the remains of a loo?'

'That he'd found the remains of a loo,' said Bellavista, smiling.

'There'd be no fortune in it for him, either!' commented Saverio.

'So let's go over it once more. When my left hand is resting on the table, not a word: it means the sucker's hooked; when I lift the mallet as high as my head, Salvatore bids; when I straighten my glasses, Saverio waits for the "two" and then bids again; and finally, when I pull out my handkerchief to mop my face, you carry on bidding for as long as you like until I put it back in my pocket. Same rates as before, ten thousand each and fifteen for the Colonel who comes in uniform, then something on top if business has been good.'

Alfredo Avitabile, auctioneer, recited the list of agreed signs in a monotone, more out of habit than anything else. He'd worked with the same assistants for more than two years and could have saved his breath: they had all the secret signs by heart. The auction room, *La Tavolozza del Golfo*[6] was known to all the inhabitants of Corso Garibaldi. No Neapolitan would ever buy a painting there, but the very opposite was true of clients from the Campanian hinterland, who seemed particularly attracted to this type of sale. Sooner or later they found themselves drawn into the room by the voice of the auctioneer relayed over loud-speakers from the auction room to the pavement outside, and once inside, the hypnotic effect of Don Alfredo's grandiloquent descriptions did the rest.

The briefing over, the little group of 'stooges' scattered strategically around the hall, four sitting in the first row of chairs, and three standing at the back to give the impression of a room packed to the gunnels. The first lot of the day was put up and the bidding started slowly and unenthusiastically. No

6 'The Palette in the Gulf'.

chicken ripe for plucking had yet appeared, hence the lack of effort.

'And now, ladies and gentlemen, I invite you to take your hats off to one of the greatest masterpieces of nineteenth-century Neapolitan painting.' Don Alfredo's voice became husky with emotion. 'Here is an early Palazzi: *Return to the Fountain*. Observe, if you will, the grace of the young peasant woman as she balances the copper jug on her head, the dark tresses of the girl, the reflections on the amphora, the exuberance of nature that seems to frame the impermanence of youth . . .'

'I've just about had enough of this *Return to the Fountain*,' Salvatore murmured to Saverio. 'If I had the money I'd buy it myself, just so that I would never have to listen again to Don Alfredo going on about the reflections on the amphora.'

'You've got a bit choosy all of a sudden!' exclaimed Saverio. 'Do what I do. I don't even hear him any more, even when we're bidding. I do it like a robot, mechanically, and wait for eight o'clock when we can take our money and go home . . .'

'Hey,' Salvatore interrupted, 'a chicken's just walked in!'

'One hundred thousand,' said Saverio immediately.

'A hundred and twenty thousand,' said Salvatore.

'A hundred and twenty thousand?' echoed Don Alfredo in tones of tragic unbelief. 'If you want to starve me out, at least be honest about it and we'll say no more! The frame alone is worth two hundred thousand lire! You may not have noticed, but this is a late nineteenth-century *guandiera*-type frame decorated with gold leaf as was fashionable in those days. To have such a frame made today – if you could find anyone capable of doing it – you would have to spend over three hundred thousand lire!'

'One hundred and forty,' said Saverio.

'One hundred and forty-five,' countered Salvatore promptly.

'One hundred and fifty,' bellowed the Colonel, raising his hand.

'One hundred and fifty-five.'

The last speaker was the *mazzone*,[7] a middle-aged man wearing

---

7 *Mazzone*: a small fish found in the Gulf of Naples that will take any bait at all, hence the equivalent of a 'sucker'.

a grey suit with a pink checked shirt and blue spotted tie that clashed violently. He had only just raised an arm and was already regretting it. Unfortunately for him, the auction, lively and competitive up to this point, immediately flagged. Don Alfredo had leant his right hand on the table and, as agreed, all bidding had ceased. Now, in an almost religious silence, the voice of the auctioneer pitilessly 'knocked down' the *Return from the Fountain*. 'One hundred and fifty-five for the first time ... One hundred and fifty-five for the second time ... One hundred and fifty-five for the third time! Congratulations, sir, you have done yourself a splendid turn and acquired a Palazzi!'

'Thanks be to Our Lady!' breathed Salvatore. 'We're shot of the *Return from the Fountain* at last!'

'Know something, Salvatò?' remarked Saverio. 'I have to admit I'm a little sorry. I'd got quite fond of the *Return from the Fountain*. Would you believe it, those reflections on the amphora were beginning to appeal to me!'

Her face scarlet with emotion, Rachelina stood in the middle of the courtyard surrounded by a a substantial group of women all trying to comfort her. As she finished relating her misadventure, she caught sight of the Professor walking towards the lift.

'Professò,' she called out, nearly in tears, 'something dreadful's just happened to me!'

'What happened?' enquired Bellavista.

'I've been robbed!'

'Handbag snatchers, eh?' said Bellavista. 'And I've warned you time and again not to carry a handbag!'

'No, Professò, this was no handbag job but a real robbery, armed robbery!'

'Armed?!'

'Yes, he was armed with a pocket-knife.'

'*Gesù, Gesù*, but anything might have happened,' commented the concierge from the block of flats opposite. 'I can understand the villains robbing rich ladies; when they see them in their furs and jewels, naturally it gives them ideas. But it's different in the case of a poor woman like Rachelina. What's the world coming to! No one's safe nowadays!'

'It was like this, Professò,' began Rachelina plaintively. 'I was on my way to do some shopping for the Finzio ladies who are, as you know, a little short of money and never want to spend very much, which is why they had given me only just the right money for what I had to buy. Well, I was on my way to the vegetable shop for two kilos of tomatoes when I suddenly felt something prick the small of my back. *Guardate ccà: m'ha scassato pure 'o vestito chillu piezzo 'e fetente!*[8]

Rachelina turned round and, to a chorus of indignant comments from her friends, showed a little tear in her dress, right at the bottom of the spine. Signora Carotenuto, a home dressmaker, immediately offered to repair it.

'Rachelì, my dear girl, *nun te preoccupà*[9]: I'll mend your dress. Come along with me and I'll do a really neat job on it. You won't even see that it was ever torn.'

'How did it happen?' asked the Professor.

'I was trying to tell you,' said Rachelina. 'When I felt the point of the knife against my back, I turned round and saw a young man I thought was a student.'

'*Nu studente?*' asked the dressmaker.

'Yes,' replied Rachelina, 'because although he had glasses he was really down at heel and no mistake. Well anyway, I turned round and he said: "Come on, hand over your money or I'll kill you!"'

'And what did you do?'

'I told him I hadn't got any on me and he said: "Then I'll kill you." I was getting frightened now and I said, "I've only got ten thousand lire", and he said, "That'll do. Give me the ten thousand." So I said, "I can't, I need it for the shopping". He thought for a moment and then said, cool as you like, "Well give me five, then", and I replied, "I can't. I've only got the one note," and he said, "Let's go and change it." So he came with

---

8 Look at this: the bastard actually tore my dress.
9 Don't worry.

me to the greengrocer's and we split it between us, five thousand each.'

'And he was holding the pocket-knife to your back all this time?' asked the dressmaker.

'Yes.'

'You were virtually conniving at the robbery!' exclaimed the Professor.

'I was that,' replied Rachelina, 'but I was nearly dying of fright!'

'In Naples, my dear Professor, a decent woman daren't go out alone any more,' commented the dressmaker, suppressing the dialect as much as possible in the presence of the professor. 'Neapolitans have all become thieves. Only yesterday, in Via Santa Lucia, the mother of a friend of mine had her handbag snatched, and they dragged her, a poor old woman of sixty, all down the road like a floor-mop!'

'That's not true, Signora. Neapolitans are no worse than any others,' said a voice with a northern accent. 'It's the same all over the world. Last year I was mugged right in the centre of Milan, and not by immigrants from the south, either.'

The man who made this latest contribution to the discussion was Doctor Cazzaniga, who had just appeared on the fringe of the group, clutching a parcel wrapped in newspaper under his arm.

'That's why I'm always on the alert whenever I've got anything of value with me,' he continued, glancing at the rudimentary package. 'Thieves are thieves wherever they are.'

'The only way of making sure you aren't robbed,' concluded Bellavista philosophically, 'is by never having anything on you that other people want.'

As the two men walked towards the lift together, Bellavista noted that, by its shape, the package Doctor Cazzaniga was carrying appeared to be a picture.

'If you don't mind my asking, have you been buying something interesting?' enquired the Professor.

'Very. You might even say that I've got a real bargain here,' the Milanese replied with a note of pride. 'I must confess that I have always been a great admirer of nineteenth-century Neapolitan painting. I believe it to be in no way inferior to the Tuscan yet until now it has been most unjustly underrated. Well, I have finally managed to acquire a painting by Antonio Mancini. A masterpiece! It's the portrait of a nurse, painted when the artist was in a mental home. Nor was it all smooth sailing, I might add, because while the man who owned it was perfectly prepared to sell, his wife was unfortunately totally opposed to it and was only persuaded with the greatest difficulty.'

In Filiberto Bonajuto's dining room a trial for fraud was in progress. Professor Bellavista and Doctor Cazzaniga, each clutching a painting, were confronting the fencing-master with indignant severity. The two portraits of the nurse were almost identical apart from the colour of the hair: Bellavista's nurse had black hair whereas Cazzaniga's was a redhead.

Signora Maria, as if nothing untoward were happening, asked her guests politely if they would like coffee.

'No thank you,' replied Bellavista coldly.

Unlike his customers, Filiberto Bonajuto was completely calm, apparently not in the least worried by the confrontation. In fact, judging by his demeanour, one would have thought the affair had nothing to do with him, and the discovery that the Mancinis were not genuine was no more than an unlucky coincidence.

'You were unfortunate. You were not supposed to meet.' This was his phlegmatic response to the complaints of the two purchasers.

'Now you listen to me,' Doctor Cazzaniga retorted calmly but firmly, 'I'm telling you for the last time that unless you reimburse us immediately, and down to the last lira, I shall have no alternative but to go to the nearest police station and denounce you as a counterfeiter.'

'That you can't do,' promptly retorted the expert in chivalric codes. 'The first thing the inspector would ask you is how much you paid for these paintings.'

'One and a half million,' said Bellavista.

'One million, seven hundred thousand,' said Cazzaniga.

'So you expected to pick up a Mancini for a million and a half? That's what the inspector would say. If you accuse me of fraud, I shall say that I told you, before accepting any money, that the paintings were merely imitations. You will have to prove to the court the likelihood of picking up a Mancini for a million and a half rather than the fifty million quoted by any reputable gallery.'

'I fear,' said Bellavista, 'that you underestimate the fact that Doctor Cazzaniga and I are both reputable professional men, whereas you, my dear Bonajuto, probably have other similar escapades on your conscience. I have, incidentally, found out that your name is not Filiberto Bonajuto but Alberto Bonaiuto, with no "j" in the surname.'

'Filiberto Bonajuto is a nom de plume.'

'Nom de paintbrush,' retorted Bellavista sarcastically.

'My dear Professor,' said a pained Bonaiuto without a j, ignoring the attack, 'what really hurts me is that you are no longer the splendid person I had the pleasure of meeting last week in this very room. How come, I ask myself, that on that occasion we conversed about art, poetry, emotion ... you explained that Art can only exist by virtue of an emotional communication between a painter and spectator who are both artists; yet now you have turned everything on its head, you talk about accusations, police inspectors! You had made such an impression on me! Look, I still have the slip of paper on which I wrote down one of your phrases ...'

Alberto Bonaiuto turned out one of his pockets and extracted a small, crumpled piece of paper.

'Here we are,' he exclaimed, and went on to read aloud in a fine declamatory style: '"In order for Art to be present in a painting, the painter must be an artist and there must be at least one spectator who is also an artist to understand him."' Raising his eyes and regarding them both sorrowfully, he then said: 'So, I'm sorry to have to say this, but neither of you gives me the impression of being an artistic spectator. You, my dear sirs, have not understood me!'

'We have understood that you have swindled us out of more than three million!' Cazzaniga remarked bitterly.

'You see, you can only talk about money,' Bonaiuto went on, more disillusioned than ever. 'And what about Emotion? What's happened to Emotion? Can't you see that I did not just sell you a couple of paintings, I sold you an Emotion too ... The Pleasure of owning a rare object ... The Frisson of ownership ... and what have you done? You smashed the Emotion like a toy to see what was inside. And now you bring the bits back to me and ask for your money back. Is that fair? Give me back the Emotion, if you will, and I shall be happy to reimburse you.'

At the end of his speech about Emotion, Don Alberto bowed like an actor taking a curtain call. He felt he had merited some applause at least for his beautifully judged delivery, and reckoned that Bellavista, in his heart of hearts, must have appreciated the performance, but he was realistic enough not to expect any outward show of approbation from his accusers. For the moment he was satisfied with the admiration of his wife who was standing beside him and gazing at him, obviously moved.

The Professor took Cazzaniga by the arm and propelled him gently towards the table for a conference.

'Dottò, let's try to be practical,' said Bellavista to his friend. 'One thing is absolutely certain: Bonaiuto has already spent our three millions.'

'I can assure you of that,' confirmed Don Alberto.

'That being so,' the Professor continued, 'the only course that makes sense is to try to save what we can.'

Then, turning to the fencing-master, he said: 'You, my esteemed friend, are now going to sign twelve promissory notes, each for two hundred and sixty-six thousand lire, to be paid punctually on the first of each month. I don't have to tell you that if one instalment is delayed by so much as a day, we shall sue you. Further, you will sign a declaration saying that you sold us two forged paintings purportedly by Antonio Mancini. You may not have noticed, but I have calculated the twelve instalments without adding any interest whatsoever.'

Bonaiuto's only reaction was to exclaim, 'Money means too

much to you, Professò! I would never have believed it. But if money is the only thing that matters to you, why do you risk it on paintings? Any painting can turn out to be a forgery, even those sold by the galleries. Remember what happened to Modigliani's heads! If you want to be certain that a picture is worth what you pay for it, go to a picture-framer, get him to make you a splendid frame and fill it with hundred-thousand banknotes. I should advise an Empire-style frame. For the record, ten millions in hundred-thousand banknotes would cover a surface measuring seventy centimetres by a hundred and fifty. Then hang it in your sitting room and all your visitors will say: "Look what a splendid picture Bellavista has got! It must be worth at least ten million!"'

'I shall withdraw the money from the bank myself,' replied Bellavista, 'so it will not even pass through your hands.'

'Regretfully, I note that I do not seem to stand very high in your esteem,' Bonaiuto remarked perspicaciously. 'And yet even this experience should have told you something about me. I am not, if you don't mind my saying so, a petty thief. Style, to my way of thinking, is everything. May I draw your attention to the fact that the sale of Mancini's *Nurse* was prepared down to the smallest detail. The whole story, to begin with, of the painter in the lunatic asylum, the friend visiting him, the brushstroke revealing madness, the volcano about to erupt ... Then the faded patch on the wall ... Professò, do you remember the faded patch on the wall? ... And finally the monologue, entitled "Papa's Mancini" in the interpretation by Maria Bonaiuto. If you would like to hear a repeat performance, it's no trouble, my wife will oblige you.' He turned to his wife: 'Maria, if I ask you very nicely, will you perform an encore for the gentlemen?'

Before either Bellavista or Cazzaniga had time to stop her, Signora Maria gathered up her hat and fox-fur from an armchair, donned them and placed herself in the doorway ready for her entrance.

'Filiberto!' she said in a quiet voice that yet thrilled with tension. 'You are selling Papa's Mancini!'

'No,' suggested the fencing-master, 'go straight to the point where you say, "You bastard, you're not going to sell the Mancini!"'

'You bastard! You're not going to sell the Mancini!' cried Signora Maria obediently. 'If you sell the Mancini, it will be over my dead body!'

'I've had enough of this farce!' announced Cazzaniga, and strode towards the door.

'Wait just a moment, Doctor,' said Bellavista, detaining him with a hand on his arm. 'He hasn't told us yet whether he's going to accept my proposal of instalments.'

The doorbell rang at that moment. Filiberto Bonaiuto, having flashed a questioning glance at his wife and received a nod of approval, said to Bellavista:

'It may be that a partial solution to our problem has turned up. Come with me to the green-room.'

'The world's a cruel place, Professò. It only appreciates Art when pain is involved,' said Bonaiuto with a sigh as he darkened his eyebrows with a stick of kohl.

The bathroom of the Bonaiuto residence was equipped like a theatre dressing-room: between the lavatory and the hand basin the 'maestro' had placed an old Neapolitan wash-stand with a marble top, and above it a large mirror with a dozen or so small lightbulbs fixed into a plain wooden frame on either side. The marble top was almost completely covered by an assortment of eyebrow-pencils, boxes of tinted foundation, burnt corks, moustaches and wigs.

Bellavista and Cazzaniga stood behind Bonaiuto and watched with interest as he peered into the mirror and started to make up. To begin with, our two buyers of the Mancini painting had been uncertain as to whether they should go straight to the police or stay to witness the performance to the end. Finally, Curiosity had proved stronger than Indignation, so there they were, watching in silence as he approved the effect of a long-haired wig.

'My wife and I alternate in the roles,' explained Bonaiuto. 'Sometimes I prepare the ground and she enters for the finale, as we did in your cases, at other times she delivers the prologue and I perform the climactic scene. Our customer today is a market gardener from Casavatore called Cascone. The friend who sent him to me says he's a very decent chap. He's apparently made a fortune out of kiwi-fruit. Have you come across kiwi-fruit? ... No? ... It's an exotic fruit that tastes of nothing at all, but it's green so people like it all the same. My agent tells me that Cascone used to work fifteen hectares of land that produced nothing but water melons and earned him very little. Then he had this brainwave about kiwi-fruit and now he's got so much money he doesn't know what to do with it. So you have every reason to feel optimistic. If the sale goes through as planned I shall be able to pay you the first instalment in about half an hour.'

'Do you intend to sell him another *Nurse*?' asked Cazzaniga sarcastically.

'Good gracious no!' replied Bonaiuto, evidently wounded by such a base insinuation. 'For the benefit of this client we have rehearsed the scene of the mad painter who destroys his canvases as soon as they are finished. Look, Doctor, it's not our fault that we have been reduced to these methods. Market forces demand suffering. A painter who is physically and mentally healthy, who doesn't take drugs, who may even get on with his wife, is a complete failure from the artistic point of view. But if he has a serious illness, is mad, dirty and on the point of death, then his value rockets, and the graver the malady, the more people ask me for his work. What do you think I should do given these circumstances?'

Alberto Bonaiuto raised his eyes and looked at Bellavista and Cazzaniga in the mirror, then, as they said nothing, he answered himself. 'I have to react to market forces. My customers want pain? I give it to them.'

'Have you ever tried to sell paintings in the normal way like any other art dealer?' asked Cazzaniga.

'Yes, but it doesn't work. You see, the problem with Modern Art is this, that because the public is incapable of appreciating a painting and forming an opinion about it, it has to judge the artist as a personality. If Salvador Dali had looked like the average man in the street, with an anonymous face and a grey suit, do you think he would have been as successful? No, my friends. You have to take the punter by the hand like a little child when it comes to choosing a picture, and that's what I'm here for, to reinforce his lack of imagination with my experience and to present him with that Feeling that he would never have had if left to his own devices. You two were merely unlucky. It was a thousand pities that you met! Otherwise, you would both, at this very moment, have been looking at your Mancinis with pride and experiencing a subtle pleasure at the sight of them hanging in your own living rooms. In your place I would keep the Mancinis even now, partly as a memento of me, partly because, speaking critically, they are very well executed. The paintings have style and intensity of expression. And you, my dear Doctor, will be returning to Milan at some stage, and from that moment the two nurses will never be in danger of meeting again . . .'

'What is your wife saying to the market gardener at this moment?' asked Bellavista.

'Are you really keen to see the performance? Would you like to witness the moment of catharsis?' Bonaiuto responded with a smile of pleasure. 'No problem. My wife will be very happy when I tell her that she had such a distinguished audience this evening. But you must be very careful not to make any noise. The living-room door is the second on the left down the passage. If you take turns at the keyhole, you will see and hear everything beautifully.'

'I don't know what to say, Don Rafè. My life is one long struggle, a constant torment. How can he, I ask myself, paint such masterpieces and then destroy them?'

Signora Maria was coming to the end of her recital for the benefit of Raffaele Cascone, the kiwi-fruit grower. The unsuspecting man listened in silence, glancing meanwhile at the latest masterpiece painted by Marvizzi, the mad painter who destroyed all his paintings.

'Believe me, Don Rafè,' the poor woman continued, 'that

man does nothing but paint all day long, sometimes not even leaving his easel for a meal, and then, as soon as he has finished the painting, he steps back a few feet, regards it with hate in his eyes and attacks it with a knife as if it were an enemy he had to kill.'

'Why don't you hide his penknives, pocket-knives or anything else that cuts?'

'That wouldn't do any good,' sighed Signora Maria. 'There are a hundred and one things about the house that could be used to cut up a picture: knives, scissors, razor blades ... Just fancy, once, he slashed a canvas – a lovely painting of a ruined building surrounded by fields – with the remote-control gadget!'

'The remote-control!' echoed the kiwi grower in astonishment. 'How did he manage that?'

'I've no idea. I only know that when he decides to destroy a canvas nothing can stop him. You see this picture here, for example? I only managed to save that by the skin of my teeth. It was nearly finished yesterday evening, he was just putting in the last poppies ...'

'Those are poppies?'

'Of course they're poppies! Can't you see? I'm surprised that a countryman like yourself should not have recognized poppies! The painting is actually called *Sunset with poppies*. So, as I was saying, he was working at his easel yesterday evening when the telephone suddenly rang. I saw my chance immediately, and said: "Sasà, that must be Colabuono. You'd better speak to him," and he went to answer it. Colabuono is an artist friend of ours who sometimes brings his paintings here for us to sell. Poor Colabuono! He's paralysed; he can only move one hand, the hand he paints with, but he's such a great artist! Some day I'll show you one of his paintings. But anyway, as I was saying, Sasà stopped painting to answer the phone and I immediately took the picture away and hid it. As you see, it's not quite finished. Here, in the left-hand corner, there are a dozen or so poppies missing.'

'And then, when he came back from answering the phone, what did he say?'

'Nothing. He's like a child. He just picked up a new canvas and started on another picture.'

'Of course, artists are extraordinary people: it's almost as if they lived in a different world!'

'Indeed, in another world. But the problem is, dear Don Rafè, that they actually live in this world, and here we have to eat, pay the rent, the electricity bill and so much else that God alone knows what it all adds up to! That is why I have to steel myself to sell his pictures.'

'Yes, Signora, I see your point, but six hundred thousand lire is too much for an unfinished picture. You yourself told me that some poppies were missing. And I've noticed something else, too: your husband hasn't signed the painting.'

'No signature?! Great God in heaven, how do you expect my husband to sign a painting? With a knife? I'll authenticate the picture myself, on the back. I'll put: "This painting is the work of my husband, Salvatore Marvizzi," and my signature. It's more important for you to remember how few of Marvizzi's paintings have ever been offered for sale; only those, in fact, that I have been able to rescue.'

'I know, but six hundred thousand is too much. Let's make it four hundred.'

'You must be joking! Four hundred thousand for Marvizzi's *Sunset with Poppies*! I'll come down fifty thousand just for you. But we must hurry, because if my husband wakes up I'll be in real trouble and you'll have missed a unique opportunity.'

At the word opportunity, the door to the passage was suddenly flung open. The painter Marvizzi, alias Marchese Filiberto Bonajuto, appeared on the threshold in all his splendour. His once-white overall was streaked with every conceivable colour, his eyes were virtual flame-throwers and his wild, unkempt, Medusa-like locks gave him the air of a horseman of the Apocalypse.

Marvizzi went straight to a writing desk, picked up a paperknife and, brandishing it like a weapon, hurled himself upon the luckless Cascone who, at that very moment, had decided to take a closer look at *Sunset with Poppies*. Signora Maria, however, managed to restrain him in time and calm him down. Marvizzi, acknowledging defeat, threw himself dejectedly into an armchair. The paper-knife fell from his hand. Signora Maria replaced it on the writing desk and said softly to Don Raffaele:

'Don Rafè, get that painting out of here. Put five hundred thousand on the desk and go!'

At the 'Tavolozza del Golfo' auction room, in the presence of Bellavista, Cazzaniga, Salvatore, Saverio, Luigino, the uniformed Colonel, Don Alberto Bonaiuto and Signora Maria, Lot 44 was just coming up.

'And here,' exclaimed the auctioneer, his voice trembling with emotion, 'we have a pair of paintings that are among the most dramatic examples of nineteenth-century art: Mancini's *Nurses*!'

# *On the Stroke of Midnight*

'Say what you like, you'll never convince me that letting off fireworks is anything but a display of barbarism! I've been living in Milan for fifteen years now, and believe me, every year, on the second of January, I am ashamed to show my face in public. Why? Because on the second of January, regular as clockwork, the *Corriere della Sera* carries the headline: ONE DEAD AND 352 INJURED IN NAPLES NEW YEAR CELEBRATIONS. But what nonsense is this, I ask myself. Naples is the home of the most enlightened minds in the whole of Italy, Giambattista Vico and Benedetto Croce – Giambattista Vico and Benedetto Croce, no less! – in the North they'd give an arm and a leg for personalities of such stature! And then we go and make ourselves a laughing stock with *tric-tracs* and *botte a muro*!'[1]

The speaker was Cardone, senior surveyor for a firm of mortgage brokers in Milan with offices at 28, Via Pirelli. He belonged to the category of southerners who speak very highly in Milan about Neapolitans but, once back in Naples, cannot find a good word for them. Cardone was at present spending Christmas in his native city, so the negative mode prevailed.

'Have you any idea how much money is spent every year on fireworks?' he asked, looking round at the assembled company.

In the ensuing silence a young man, his face pinched with cold, appeared in the doorway of the bar and called out:

'Any chance of a *sospeso*?'

'You're in luck, Alfò,' replied the barman. 'Ericuccio was here only ten minutes ago and left a *sospeso*. I gather that his landlord,

[1] Types of firework. Firecrackers and thunderflashes.

Avvocato Capuozzo, took a tumble on the ice this morning and Ericuccio felt like celebrating.'

The *sospeso* is an old Neapolitan tradition now all but extinct. You will only find it still observed in a few bars in the poorer quarters. Here, when a customer has some special reason for celebrating, he pays not only his own consumption but leaves a coffee 'in the pipe' for a future customer. This is called a *sospeso* and is a way of virtually inviting the whole of humanity to have a coffee on you.

'*Assa fà à Madonna!*[2] That's the first good news I've heard this week,' exclaimed Alfonso Cannavale, rubbing his hands together partly from satisfaction at having found a *sospeso*, partly to restore the circulation.

The man had no overcoat, and the collar of his slightly threadbare jacket was turned up to protect his neck. His style of dress caused some raised eyebrows, since the roads that morning were icy and Vesuvius completely covered with snow. Individuals with no overcoat are a common enough sight in Naples in the depths of winter, yet it can be colder than anywhere else in Italy. Someone once started the rumour that this city enjoys a mild climate and the advent of cold weather invariably takes the Neapolitans as much by surprise as if it were a completely unforeseeable Act of God.

'Shall I tell you who are the only remaining people who still celebrate the New Year with fireworks?' Cardone continued relentlessly. 'Ourselves, the Mexicans and a few tribes in Central Africa. That says it all.'

'You're quite right,' said the barman, 'but the police have completely forbidden *botte a muro* this year. Only the other day they raided Porta Capuana and sequestrated over six hundred kilos of fireworks.'

'Six hundred kilos? What are six hundred kilos? Six tons would have been nearer the mark! Six hundred kilos is nothing!' exploded Cardone furiously. 'Forgive me for repeating myself, but as fellow-citizens of Giambattista Vico

---

[2] 'Blessed be our Lady!' (Neapolitan dialect.)

and Benedetto Croce, we cannot behave like barbarians!'

'May I say something?' asked Alfonso Cannavale, the man without an overcoat. 'I agree with you that some fireworks are dangerous, but don't throw out the baby with the bathwater. There are different kinds of fireworks, *fuochi da rumore*, the ones that go off with a bang, and *fuochi di colore*, those that just look pretty, and the latter are completely harmless. And even some of the loud ones aren't dangerous if you take the simplest precautions. Take *tric-tracs*, for example. If you remove the final bang, which means you don't get the big explosion that causes the damage, you're only left with the little pops, but at least no one gets hurt. To abolish all fireworks seems way over the top to me! If we can't even have a few Roman candles on New Year's Eve, what have we got left?'

'So,' retorted Cardone with a malicious look at Alfonso, 'you don't think it matters if we end up this year, as before, with the odd death and four or five hundred people injured?'

'Now you're exaggerating: that wasn't what I said,' protested Alfonso. 'If a man starts blasting away with a pistol and kills someone, he's a criminal no matter what day of the year it happens to be, New Year's Eve or any other. But tradition has its place, too. For instance, when I came out this morning, my children were pleading with me: "Papa, bring us some bangers," they said. What can I do? Go home empty-handed? How could I face them? The real problem, my friend, is rather different: I haven't even got the money to buy ten *fuggi-fuggi* and a packet of sparklers!'

*Fuggi-fuggi* and sparklers both belong to the *fuochi di colore* variety: they are cheap and completely harmless. Especially sparklers which, being only wires dipped in sulphur, send out hundreds of tiny twinkling stars, ideal for parents to give their small children to keep them happy and make sure they stay well away from the more dangerous varieties.

'Listen to me!' cried Cardone, turning on the unfortunate Alfonso. 'Just tell me what makes it imperative for you to have fireworks. There. That's what I want to know: *why must you have fireworks?*'

'For crying out loud, we've always had fireworks on New Year's Eve in Naples to bring good luck in the coming year. New Year's Eve is New Year's Eve!'

'So explain something else,' continued Cardone, forgetting that he too was born in Naples. 'You Neapolitans, the more hunger and unemployment you have, the more you want to celebrate. Take yourself, for example. You've just told me you're broke. Right. Now tell me what you intend to celebrate and why you feel so festive!'

'I can tell you that at once,' said Alfonso quietly. 'My fireworks are a personal protest and, since the Almighty has been deaf to my prayers, I'm hoping that on New Year's Eve the noise at least will get through to him.'

'I see, now we're dragging in the Almighty who, you say, is deaf!'

'Not deaf as such, but certainly indifferent,' said Alfonso, qualifying his statement. 'The truth is, that after a year of misery like the one I've just lived through, any poor devil would feel relieved to see the back of it, hoping that the next one will be better.'

'I don't know how much you're going to spend on fireworks this evening,' retorted Cardone mercilessly, 'but in your shoes, forgive me for speaking so frankly, I'd be saving up for an overcoat.'

There was no getting round the fact that Alfonso Cannavale had, at all costs, to find the minimum necessary to celebrate the New Year. Forty thousand lire would be enough, even thirty thousand if the family did without fish as a main course: twenty for the meal and ten for the fireworks. But how to earn thirty thousand? First he tried Signora Sangiorgio, offering to clean the steps of the building in Via San Biagio dei Librai from top to bottom. But the widow told him to come back after Twelfth Night. Then he asked his brother-in-law for a loan, but the only response was a kick in the pants. His last hope was Cavaliere Santillo for whom he had worked as an errand boy for ten years. Now eighty, the Cavaliere no longer owned the stationery wholesale business at the Rettifilo (three adjoining shops, one on the corner of Via Pietro Colletta). He had sold it piecemeal, first one shop, then another, then another. He still sold exercise books, pens and pencils from a tiny cubby-hole one metre thirty by four metres in the passage-way running down the side of his former premises. To compensate for the reduction of space, he himself had grown smaller: at eighty, he had shrunk.

'Alfonsì,' the Cavaliere had said, 'I'm very fond of you as you know, but I cannot give you any money. The only reason I keep open is force of habit. Once the academic year is over, no one comes here any more. These days customers prefer the big stores where they feel free, where they can handle the goods and walk around. Tell me: where would they walk around here?'

Evening found Alfonso in Piazza San Gaetano, where he had been sitting for three hours in the hope that someone would ask him to do a job, labouring, plumbing or anything else. But the hours had gone by and no one had asked him to do anything. Naples seemed intent upon the evening's celebrations and nothing else. Men and women hurried by, each one clutching a small parcel.

Alfonso Cannavale could have told you exactly what each package contained. It all depends, he would have said, on the way it's carried. If someone dangles a plastic bag from a couple of fingers and swings it in a casual sort of way, you can be sure it's only ordinary foodstuffs: vegetables, meat, cheese and suchlike. If, on the other hand, they glance at the plastic bag from time to time, the chances are that there's an eel inside. An eel, if alive, demands a measure of attention and the person carrying it is obliged to check up on it from time to time. Then if you see a gentleman clasping a package under his arm, and maybe even protecting it with his other hand, you can bet it's a present of some value. Finally, if the package is borne in both hands, like a tray, it can only be one of two things, pastries or fireworks. It would be simply too dangerous to clasp fireworks under your arm or swing them in a plastic carrier bag, especially if there should happen to be the odd *botta a muro* among the *tric-tracs*.

All in all, the only faces to be seen that evening were merry ones. Lucky people, mused Alfonso, not to have problems. But among the hundreds of people passing by, he had not found one from whom he would venture to ask for a loan of thirty thousand lire. It crossed his mind to approach Professor Bellavista, whose face was the only friendly one he saw in three hours of waiting, but then his courage failed him. Bellavista was a teacher of Philosophy and paid no attention to anniversaries of any kind.

'Alfò,' he had said to him last year, in reply to his New Year greeting, 'you say that today is the 31 December, but I'm not so sure about it. If Gregory XIII had minded his own business in 1582, today would be only 20 December and New Year would fall on 11 January. But don't think that the Gregorian reform is the end of the matter. Every one hundred years the calendar is out by sixty-one ten-millionths of a day, not to mention the Buddhists, who celebrate the New Year on 12 January. For myself, if you must know, I don't even agree with the decision of the Council of Nicaea to fix the equinox on 21 March, so shall I tell you what I'm planning to do? At half past eleven tonight, I'm going to bed!'

How could one possibly ask for a loan from a person who thought like that? And what, after all, was there to celebrate? No, he might as well give up. Fate had decreed that this year should end as it had begun, in grinding poverty. Only the thought of his children made the financial impossibility of fireworks so bitter for Alfonso, for they had been counting on him.

'I'd have been a hundred times better off had I stayed in America,' he thought. 'I wouldn't be in this situation now. OK, I went hungry there, too, but that was American hunger, not Italian! In New York the relief cheque for an unemployed worker pays three hundred thousand a week, more or less the salary of a Council clerk after ten years' service! The word "hunger" conjures up God knows what ideas in our minds, but we have to be more exact, and ask "hunger where?" Because hunger means one thing in America, another in Italy and yet another in Ethiopia. What's important is to choose a country that has an acceptable kind of hunger.'

\*

A banner bore the following legend in huge letters: ANDREA 'O CRIMINALE, FIREWORK KING: NO FOOLING ABOUT, NO BAD BEHAVIOUR TOLERATED. Down both sides of the booth ran borders of coloured fireworks interlaced with Roman candles. In one corner was a life-size portrait of Diego Maradona surrounded by cardboard tubing subdivided sausage-like into sections stuffed with gunpowder. The footballer's head was haloed with a Catherine wheel.

'How much are Roman candles?' asked Alfonso.

'One thousand for the little ones, two thousand for the two-colour ones and three thousand for the white, red and green,' replied Andrea *'o criminale* drily.

'And the rockets without a bang?'

'The ones you stand in a bottle?'

'Yes, those.'

'Three thousand if you buy only one, two thousand each if you buy ten.'

'Ah ... I'd like a dozen *tofè*,' said Alfonso as if he really had the money in his pocket. 'How much is a *tofa*?'

'A *tofa* or a *tofa-tofa*?' Andrea enquired.

'A *tofa*.'

'Five hundred lire and the whistle is guaranteed.'

'And a set-piece of twelve bangers?'

'Young man,' exclaimed *'o criminale*, his patience wearing thin, 'tell me the truth: are you conducting an enquiry into the price of fireworks, or do you actually intend to buy something?'

''Onn 'Andrè,' replied Alfonso humbly, 'to tell the truth, I've got a little cash-flow problem at the moment and wanted to get a general idea about prices.'

'How much can you afford to spend altogether? Tell me and I'll see that you impress the neighbours.'

'How can I put this ... I can't spend very much ...'

'I get the drift. You've not got a lira in your pocket!'

'That's just it, but if you allow me credit, I could pay you back in a week's time.'

'Young man,' replied *'o criminale* with a sigh, 'I'd do it if I could, but believe me, if I was in the business of giving a week's credit, by now the Neapolitans would have cleaned out the whole stall. Before he died, my father told me: "My boy, once a firework has been used it is nothing but a wisp of smoke and a handful of ash, and debts go the same way." '

'OK, but we're only talking about very limited credit.'

'What can I say? You're unlucky. This year the Japanese have flooded the market with a whole mass of fireworks cheaper and more spectacular than ours. Even the tobacconists are selling them. Our *fuochi da rumore* are still better than theirs, but they've wiped the board where the others are concerned. To put it in a nutshell, we're in a crisis situation.'

'But what are the Neapolitan factories doing about it?'

'Producing fake Japanese fireworks. They buy the paper printed with little flowers direct from Japan, stamp them Made in Japan and sell them as authentic.'

'And how do you suggest I save my face this evening?'

'Young man, I can only repeat that I never give credit. It's an old company rule. The only thing I can give you is some technical advice. If you've got five thousand lire, buy one *botta a muro*, but be sure it's a big one, a gigantic one, a veritable atomic bomb. Apart from that, from what you've told me, I don't see you've got a choice. To impress the neighbours you'd have to spend at least three hundred thousand lire. In Naples today, if you spend less than three hundred thousand lire you're nobody! But the bang I'm talking about is beyond price, it'll make your name.'

Alfonso entered his home without a glance for his wife or children. Producing a litre of milk, half a barbecued chicken and a few slices of pizza from a brown paper bag, he set them down on the table and said:

'I'm not hungry, you eat. I'm going to bed.'

'Alfò, love,' said his wife imploringly and almost in tears, 'stay and eat with us.'

'Papa, no bangers?' asked the younger of the two children, 'No sparklers?'

'Eat your supper and then straight to bed!' ordered Alfonso in the kind of voice that pre-empted any argument. 'Fireworks are only fit for barbarians! Every year they cause death and injuries and we get criticized by everybody else, including Benedetto Croce! You're only little so you're still young enough to avoid traditions. I'd rather you learned to behave like civilized people. Forget about celebrations and fireworks! In this house there is nothing to celebrate.'

'But Papa,' complained Rafiluccio, the elder of the two, 'it's New Year's Eve!'

'We can't even be sure about that,' said Alfonso, on his way to the bedroom. 'It may be 20 December.'

'Then why do people let off bangers?'

'Because they don't know any better.'

Gigino, the litle one, started to whimper. Alfonso, pretending not to notice, undressed in silence and climbed into bed. There was only one bedroom, with a double bed against the long wall and a single one at the foot of it for the children. Half an hour later, Alfonso's wife and the children also came to bed. They undressed and lay down but no one slept. Every now and then Gigino's sobs were heard in the dark.

Even without looking at the clock, Alfonso could tell exactly how many minutes it was to midnight.

Five minutes, four, three, two, one ... midnight! Alfonso lay as if turned to stone, his eyes on the ceiling, saying nothing. Giuseppina longed to give him a kiss but realized that this was not the moment, that tonight he was best left alone. The children were awake, too. Rafiluccio sat in the middle of the bed, watching his father silently with eyes that were moist with tears.

PUM, PUM, TA TA PAM, PUM, TA TA TA TA TA ... PUM. Naples, as usual, was going mad. Explosions followed each other without a pause. No one who was not in the trenches during the First World War can imagine what Naples is like on New Year's Eve. From time to time a tremendous crash shook the walls of the room. Intermittent flashes and reflections lit up the whitewashed windows, illuminating Alfonso's face as he stared up at the ceiling.

A rhythmic series of a dozen or so bangs rattled the window panes harder than before.

'That's a twelve-burst aerial shell,' remarked Alfonso almost in a whisper. 'Last year that cost two thousand lire, but today *'o criminale* was asking three thousand. God alone knows what they'll be next year.'

The window was suddenly suffused with green, then red then white once more.

'That's Ragioniere D'Alessandro; he's gone for a tricolour "waterfall" again. What I want to know is where he gets all that money. He works for the Council, cemeteries department. How on earth could anyone nick all that money from the cemeteries department? If you calculate that every coloured Bengal light costs three thousand, and he puts twenty of them in each row ... three times twenty is sixty ... sixty times three thousand is a hundred and eighty thousand lire! Jesus!'

A mighty explosion rocked the room.

'Aha,' Alfonso continued, 'that must be the "atomic bomb" Andrea *'o criminale* was talking about this evening. Don Carmine Anzalone, I should think. With that ironmongery business of his he must earn more than enough for such things. Nothing from the right: Bebè Janelli hasn't begun yet. He wants to finish last, as usual. Idiot. He thinks no one notices that he starts after everybody else: last year the first *tracco* went off at half-past midnight. I just don't understand some people. If you can't compete with the big boys like Anzalone and Coppola, then give in gracefully and at least keep your self-respect. Set off the fireworks you've got and don't make a fool of yourself!'

Three small bangs were followed by a great boom, more small bangs and finally a whole series of whistles each ending with a sharp crack.

*'Mamma mia bella!'* exclaimed Alfonso, who had kept up his running commentary for over ten minutes now. 'Coppola's really on the attack, and Anzalone's returning his fire blow for blow. Janelli's taking advantage of the situation and saving up for the finale. Ragioniere D'Alessandro's letting them get on with it. Quite right too. He won't buy anything except *fuochi di colore*. Once the last Bengal lights have gone, that's it and he shuts up the balcony. I haven't heard anything yet from Ingegnere

Castorino who works in the civil engineer's office ... shouldn't be difficult to make something on the side there ... you'd expect more, logically, from Castorino than from D'Alessandro. Those *tric-tracs* come from Caradonna, the deputy mayor: rubbishy things, three hundred lire each. And here comes Don Carmine Anzalone's grand finale. I recognize it: *tofe* and *botte al muro*, alternating: whistle and bang, whistle and bang!'

The noise continued without a pause. Alfonso was concentrating on identifying a series of bangs in the distance when he became aware of the children's muffled sobs. Propelled by a wave of anger, he leaped out of bed, snatched the little ones from their bed and carried them across to the picture of the Madonna of Pompeii.

'*Guagliù!*'[3] cried Alfonso, his eyes blazing as he placed a hand on the picture. 'I swear to you by this beautiful Madonna of Pompeii that as soon as Papa makes some money, he'll fire a salvo that will be the talk of Naples for years to come!'

Commissario[4] Di Domenico had been stationed in Naples for some time. On this morning, as on every other, the first thing he did on getting to his office was prepare himself a cup of coffee in the bathroom, where he had installed a small electric ring, a coffee-maker and everything he needed for four cups of coffee a day.

'The bars keep putting their prices up and they can go to hell,' he said to his friends. 'But we'll see which of us has the last laugh!'

He was still enjoying his coffee when his sergeant, Colapietro, came in.

'Sir, there's a certain Cannavale waiting outside. We arrested him last night for disturbing the peace during the hours of darkness. What shall I do? Shall I get him in?'

'What has he done?' asked the Commissario.

'He was setting off fireworks, *tric-tracs* and *botte a muro* just as

---

3 Boys. (Neapolitan dialect)
4 *Commissario*: Equivalent grade to Inspector.

if it were New Year's Eve. All the neighbours have complained.'

'And you arrested him for that? A warning would have been enough.'

'I know, but the fact is, we had a call from ...' replied Colapietro and whispered a name.

'Ah, I see,' sighed Di Domenico, rolling his eyes up to the ceiling. 'Very well, then. Let's have him in and question him. Incidentally, Colapietro, before I forget, the bulb's gone in the bathroom. Fix a new one but don't throw the old one away as I've got a use for it.'

Colapietro replaced the bulb and returned a minute later with Alfonso.

'Sit there,' said the sergeant.

Alfonso Cannavale sat down and waited. He had passed an unforgettable night: what a salvo! Triple-headed rockets, one after another and the entire population of Via Luigi Settembrini hanging out of its windows watching. Very satisfactory! Rafiluccio and Gigino, dressed in their confirmation suits, each in charge of ten red, white and green Bengal lights and two whirling Catherine wheels. In the space of twenty minutes the Cannavale family had sent up four hundred thousand lire's worth of fireworks, bought direct from the factory in San Pietro a Patierno at clearance sale prices. The finale had consisted of five *botte a muro*, Hiroshima type. Alfonso was convinced that those *botte a muro* must have been heard as far away as Piazza Garibaldi. Then the arrival of the police: 'Who's that?' 'Police.' 'What's the matter?' 'We're taking you in.'

The Commissario had not so much as looked at Cannavale yet. First he went to the bathroom, locked himself in, stayed there for a couple of minutes, flushed the cistern and then returned to the office carrying a light bulb which he deposited in the drawer of his desk.

'Here's the statement,' said Colapietro, seating himself behind an ancient typewriter.

Di Domenico took the statement and placed it on his desk, then took out his glasses and cleaned them with a piece of chamois he kept in the middle drawer. Alfonso believed the moment had come to speak, but Commissario Di Domenico apparently had more preliminaries to attend to before starting his day's work. He picked up the stub of a pencil no longer than 3 centimetres, sharpened it with a razor blade and fixed it into a tin holder that enabled him to use it right down to the end. And then, at last, he read the statement, signed it with the pencil, put it down on the right of the desk, looked at Alfonso and, as if continuing a discussion already in progress, said:

'So, in the middle of the night, you started letting off fireworks!'

'Middle of the night? I began at midnight on the dot, the traditional time,' Alfonso protested.

'What tradition? The twelfth of January?'

'Exactly, Commissario, the twelfth of January. I'm a Buddhist!'

'Cannavà,' retorted the Commissario, his tone hardening, 'if you intend to start cracking jokes at eight o'clock in the morning, feel free; I won't stop you; on the contrary, I'll send you to crack a few more in Poggioreale.'[5]

'I'm not joking, I only meant that different religions observe the New Year on different dates.'

'Very well, but other religions are not in the habit of celebrating the New Year with fireworks. You were letting off fireworks. Wasn't New Year's Eve enough for you?'

'No, because then I didn't let off a single firework. I didn't have any money.'

'That's no excuse for letting them off on 12 January.'

'It's easy enough for you to say that, but try explaining it to my children! I tried my level best to do what was expected of me but nothing went right. All I managed, and that only just, was some milk and half a barbecued chicken. Try to understand, Commissario. That evening, in my children's eyes, I was a failure!'

'You can't mean that!' exclaimed the Commissario. 'A failure! Doing what's expected of you! You Neapolitans are all crazy; if a man can't let off fireworks at midnight, he's immediately

---

[5] A Naples prison.

regarded as a failure! I didn't have fireworks this year either, but that doesn't mean I regard myself as a failure.'

'No fireworks?' asked Alfonso incredulously.

'No,' replied Di Domenico, adding: 'As a protest against the rising cost of fireworks, I refused to buy any at all. All I did was to throw out of the window some old electric light bulbs I'd collected in the course of the year. They made a noise just the same and didn't cost me a single lira.'

'Old light bulbs?'

'Exactly, old light bulbs. If you think I'm not telling the truth, see here,' said the Commissario, taking the light bulb from the drawer where he had just put it. 'I got this one this morning.'

'Very well,' said Alfonso in a conciliatory tone, 'but it's not a serious crime to set off a few fireworks!'

'That's what you say, young man. The law, however, says otherwise. Just a moment, and I'll read it to you.'

The Commissario leafed rapidly through a statute book lying on his desk.

'So ... let's see ... Article 685 ... no, that's acts of sedition ... here we are, Article 703: "Whoever shall, without the relevant permission from the authorities, in a residential area or a place near a residential area or upon the public highway or in the direction of the same, let off firearms or fire rockets or launch aerostats by means of combustion..."'

'Launch what?'

'Aerostats ... hot-air balloons, weather balloons.'

'I didn't do that.'

'I know, but the law has to cover all eventualities. And here's the bit that concerns you: "... or let off fireworks, or in general cause combustions or explosions likely to endanger life, shall be liable to a fine of forty thousand lire and up to one month's detention." Cannavà, forty thousand lire and up to one month's detention!'

'That seems a bit steep!' exclaimed Alfonso in amazement. 'A month's detention, just for celebrating a successful business deal! But who filed the complaint?'

'A neighbour of yours.'

'I see. I'll bet it was that bastard Bebè Janelli. Believe me, Commissario, that man's capable of selling his own grandmother!'

'No, it wasn't Janelli.'

'Who, then? D'Alessandro? Anzalone? Coppola?'

'All right, I'll tell you and set your mind at rest. Once you know who you're dealing with, you'll be more careful in future. You, my dear Cannavale, happen to live directly opposite my immediate superior, Mr Deputy Mayor Caradonna. It was he who filed the complaint. That's why I can't just ignore it. What can I say? You're just unlucky!'

'Commissario,' Alfonso enquired, pointing to the statute book, 'just now, when you were reading out Article ...'

'703.'

'... Article 703, I don't seem to remember anything about fireworks let off on 31 December being an exception.'

'No, the law makes no exceptions.'

'Then, with your permission, I wish to file a complaint against my neighbour, Vicequestore Caradonna, who, on 31 December last, in Via Settembrini and in the direction of the said street, let off about twenty nimminy-pimminy *tric-tracs* costing three hundred lire apiece, preventing the legitimate slumbers of myself and my family in the dead of night.'

'Very well, Cannavà, I see what you're getting at,' said Di Domenico, rising from his desk and indicating that the interview was over. 'Sign a receipt for the statement and get the hell out of here.'

The officer was about to put a new sheet of paper in his typewriter when Di Domenico stopped him.

'Colapiè, what are you doing? Wasting paper? Use the statement we've got, write on the back and get him to sign it!'

# Socrates and the Bumper Question

SOCRATES My dear Phaedrus, where have you come from and where are you going?

PHAEDRUS I have been with Lysias, the son of Cephalus, O Socrates, and now I am going for a walk outside the city walls because I have decided to buy a second-hand car and I wish to look at an Auto-Mart that has recently opened, so I've been told, on the way to Eleusis.

SOCRATES But having decided to buy a car, why not wait until you have enough money for a new one?

PHAEDRUS Not being an experienced driver as yet, I prefer to learn on a second-hand model. But tell me, Socrates, why, despite having the funds, have you still not bought a car?

SOCRATES What would I need a car for?

PHAEDRUS To go wherever you wanted to go.

SOCRATES And where would that be?

PHAEDRUS Oh, I don't know ... To the agora, for example, since, living as you do in the deme of Alopece, you have a half-hour walk every morning ...

SOCRATES And you think I find all this walking distasteful?

PHAEDRUS Surely I do, O Socrates.

SOCRATES As a matter of fact, dear Phaedrus, I enjoy walking so much that if I were exceedingly rich and owned a motor car, to avoid sacking my chauffeur I would hand the car over to him and ask him to follow me, step for step. Do you not realize that riding in a car would completely destroy every chance of meeting my friends, of stopping and chatting to them?

PHAEDRUS What you say may well be justified where short distances are concerned, but not long ones. Without a car, how can you reach the faraway places worth visiting in a reasonable time?

SOCRATES Xenophanes, so I'm told, spent seventy years travelling the length and breadth of the world and even reached the far distant town of Elea, yet he never, as far as I know, owned even a humble Fiat 500. But if we allow, simply for the sake of a good argument, that a car is indispensable for seeing the world, can you give me one sound reason for wanting to see it?

PHAEDRUS Well really! To look around you, to enjoy the beauties of nature. Have you ever seen the peaks around Pilos? The cliffs and chasms of Cythera? The olive groves that bedeck the slopes of lovely Thessaly? Would you want to die without seeing all this beauty?

SOCRATES Don't be angry with me, Phaedrus, but the most important thing to me is learning. What could cliffs and trees and fields possibly have to teach me, especially when there is so much I can still learn from men? And where men are concerned, I think there are enough in Athens to make it unnecessary to go around hunting for more. But now I have a misgiving which I should like to share with you.

PHAEDRUS Speak freely, without reticence.

SOCRATES I have the impression that car-owners, as a breed, are not all that susceptible to the beauties of nature. Never, in fact, have I seen one of them pull off the road to admire the scenery. Their only ambition, it seems to me, is to get from A to B, covering a particular distance in an allotted space of time.

PHAEDRUS You speak truly, O Socrates. But see, here comes Aristogamus. As you know, he is an Alfa Romeo executive, so he may be able to shed some light on the topic.

ARISTOGAMUS What subject are you discussing, my friends, and what is your point of disagreement?

PHAEDRUS I am about to purchase a car, because I believe it to be indispensable, but Socrates is arguing that cars are good for nothing.

SOCRATES I would find one useful if I had the misfortune to be paralysed and did not have the use of my legs.

ARISTOGAMUS You won't get anywhere with Socrates, my dear Phaedrus, by talking about Progress. Knowing as you do his sympathetic attitude towards the Cynics and Antisthenes, how do you imagine that he, who has yet to discover the use of shoes, could accept the necessity for cars? Socrates knows nothing – or perhaps prefers to know nothing – about Progress and the way it has changed the way men live.

SOCRATES I believe that nothing invented by this new god you call Progress is actually more than some kind of 'extension'. The motor car is an extension of legs, the telephone an extension of ears, the television of eyes and the computer of the brain. But as far as I know, not one of these new inventions has ever been able to change the essential nature of man. Years go by, in fact, and despite all these extensions that keep coming on to the market, men continue to behave in exactly the same way as before. Are there not still men as ambitious as Alcibiades, as jealous as Menelaus, as envious as Thyestes? When the day comes, as I hope it will, that Progress is able to manufacture Love and Liberty at a price all can afford, then I, my dear Aristogamus, will be one of his most fervent devotees.

ARISTOGAMUS My dear Socrates, your head is always in the clouds. Aristophanes is quite right to make fun of you. If it were up to you, men would still be sleeping in trees and wearing animal skins.

SOCRATES Since I fear that you underrate the perils of Progress, I should like to tell you something I heard from Parmenides that day when I met him in Pythodorus' house. Slightly to the north of Elea there is, apparently, a big coastal city called Neapolis, very charming and very populous. So beloved of Zeus was Neapolis that its bay, so I'm told, is the loveliest in the world. Several islands of outstanding beauty surround it like a necklace of diamonds encircling the throat of an oriental queen, and the sky is even bluer than the eyes of Glaucus. Vulcan himself, they say, contributed to this landscape by causing one of his forges, a mountain named Vesuvius, to belch forth lava and so help to conserve the archaeological remains of Pompeii and Herculaneum for posterity. For all these reasons Neapolis became, for two centuries, one of the favourite spots for visitors from all over the world. The English even devised a saying for it, 'See Naples and die', meaning that there is little point in continuing to live once one has seen the most beautiful sight nature ever created.

ARISTOGAMUS Why are you telling us these things, O Socrates, and what is the connection between the beauty of Neapolis and the usefulness of the motor car?

SOCRATES If you will be patient, my dear friend, I shall show you how this tin can on four wheels, which you call a motor car, has a potential for power greater than that of Zeus and Vulcan rolled into one.

PHAEDRUS Tell us anything you like, Socrates, for we are listening.

SOCRATES As I was saying, Neapolis used to be a target for tourists and scholars alike until, quite suddenly, all the travel companies dropped it from their itineraries on account of the motor car. Put off by the chaotic conditions on the roads, the din of horns and the traffic jams that make it impossible to move freely from one end of the city to the other, today's tourists refuse to stay in the hotels and the only part of the city they see is that lying between the airport and the hydrofoil terminus.

ARISTOGAMUS And you believe that if motor cars were eliminated, Neapolis would flourish once more?

SOCRATES I am absolutely convinced of it. And for another reason as well, which is that Neapolis suffers from a further affliction, the Camorra.

PHAEDRUS The Camorra? What is that, a disease?

SOCRATES In a certain sense yes, my dear Phaedrus, it is a social sickness that can even be fatal. The Camorra is an association of bandits who extort money and terrorize the entire city.

ARISTOGAMUS But what has the Camorra got to do with motor cars?

SOCRATES I hardly need explain that bandits could not operate without motor cars, since the finale to each and every criminal exploit is the get-away. In other words, you cannot rob a bank and then wait for a bus. Indeed, the more barren a man's soul and the greater tendency he has to bad taste, the more he cannot do without a motor car. I can give you a concrete example to illustrate my point. Just off the coast of Neapolis there are two islands called Capri and Ischia. Since the roads are so narrow, no cars at all are allowed on the former, and because of this the visitors are all cultured and refined; in the case of the latter, however, the situation is reversed: although the natural beauty of the scenery is just as splendid, the island is invaded every summer by hordes of motorized hooligans who render it uninhabitable. In the light of such considerations, I maintain that all the problems that beset Neapolis could be solved at a stroke if the use of the motor car were forbidden within the city boundaries and only public transport allowed. The criminals would take themselves off and the tourists, no longer disturbed by the noise of the traffic, would return in droves to this Paradise regained.

ARISTOGAMUS Do you think that Athens too is in danger of being beset with similar problems?

SOCRATES Yes, of that I am sure, unless restrictions upon the movement of vehicles are imposed immediately.

PHAEDRUS In all probability, O Socrates, you are right. However, since I have had to put up with shanks's pony for twenty years while watching others drive round in their cars, I reckon it's my turn now to experience the thrill of speed for the next twenty years at least. When I have exercised my right where this is concerned, I may come round to your way of thinking.

SOCRATES I fear, my dear friend, that you will find it a little difficult to experience the thrill of speed in Athens. Have you not noticed that it becomes more difficult every day to make your way through the centre of the old town?

ARISTOGAMUS As the wisest of us all, what measures would you recommend to the transport *strategoi* for improving the flow of traffic through our city?

SOCRATES I should recommend lanes for the exclusive use of well-utilized vehicles.

ARISTOGAMUS Well-utilized in what sense?

SOCRATES I would penalize solitary drivers. When I leave my house every morning I notice that nearly every car that passes me carries a single person: the driver. This means that the Athenians, practically speaking, leave home and carry around with them several hundreds of thousands of cubic metres of air. My plan, however, would provide that in all the busier parts of the city, especially in the centre of the Old Town, only cars carrying a minimum of three people would be allowed. Such a regulation would mean that office-workers would be persuaded to commute to their places of work in groups of three, an excellent boost for the art of conversation and for human understanding.

ARISTOGAMUS I fear that it would only encourage the birth of a new profession, that of the hired passenger.

PHAEDRUS Incidentally, Aristogamus, how come that you are alone today? Where's your friend Meneandrus?

ARISTOGAMUS The very reason I came to the colonnade of Zeus the Liberator is that I arranged to meet him here.

PHAEDRUS Have you already decided on a programme for the rest of the day, or can you stay and converse with us?

ARISTOGAMUS No. Meneandrus is going to pick me up in his car, a Land-Rover, and take me to a restaurant in the Phalerum where, he says, the fish is excellent.

SOCRATES I saw Meneandrus this very morning, washing his car in a little open space just by the temple of Artemis. I doubt if he ever lavished as much care on himself or on his own wife, poor Calymno. When he had finished drying the car with a cloth of Tyrian purple, he stepped back a few paces to admire it better, then returned to it and caressed every curve and crevice as gently as though it were the body of his lover. I have seen many slaves do such work, but I've never before seen a decent Athenian gentleman so occupied. It was obvious from the way he touched the car that he was deriving exquisite pleasure from the contact, such as the priests of Pallas must feel when they are permitted to touch the statue of the Goddess.

PHAEDRUS Many people in Athens love their cars in this way, O Socrates. I can't imagine why you should be so surprised.

SOCRATES I am sorry to disappoint you, my dear Phaedrus, but I really cannot understand such an emotion. I admit my limitations: I admire Phryne's breasts and I can yield to the lust of the flesh when I look upon the body of Clinias' young son, but I doubt whether I should ever find a Land-Rover more desirable than Phryne or Alcibiades.

ARISTOGAMUS Every generation has its own fetishes, its myths. Maybe, my dear Socrates, you are simply growing old.

SOCRATES But come, Aristogamus, you, as a man working in the car industry, why do you not get down to designing some improvements to this dreadful machine, the motor car?

ARISTOGAMUS Why do you think it should be improved? The motor car of today is the peak of perfection.

SOCRATES Not at all. I think the whole thing is misconceived and I can prove it if you have the time to hear me out.

ARISTOGAMUS As I said, I'm waiting for Meneandrus. Meanwhile, I've got nothing to do so I might as well listen to your imagination running wild.

SOCRATES The major defect of every motor car is the inadequacy of its bumpers.

ARISTOGAMUS The bumpers? Why on earth?

SOCRATES Because the way they are designed makes them not a line of defence, which is what I presume they should be, but a weapon of attack, to the point where it would be more logical to call them 'crashers'.

ARISTOGAMUS Explain that more fully, O Socrates!

SOCRATES As I see it, the law should require that all bumpers be at the same height off the ground so that they can perform their proper function more efficiently. Otherwise, the bumpers of one car dent the bodywork of another car and the bumpers of the second car dent the bodywork of a third vehicle. Am I not right, O Phaedrus?

PHAEDRUS Quite right, O Socrates.

SOCRATES These matters should really be raised by Pericles himself when he is summoned to take his place among the representatives of the United Nations. Since this international organization and others like it seem incapable of dealing with the big problems, at least they could address the small ones. To do its work properly, a bumper must always strike against a bumper. If this is not the case then it acts like the beak that Gaius Duilius had fitted to the prow of Roman vessels to enable them to sink the Carthaginians. Now, seeing that we are designing the car of the future, allow me to describe all the innovations I should like to see.

PHAEDRUS Speak, O Socrates, for your suggestions will be most useful to people like myself who are contemplating the purchase of a car.

SOCRATES One: A car should only be designed to carry two people and should be no longer than the width of our present models so that it can always be parked with its nose to the kerb. A great many people believe that a big car is more comfortable than a small one, whereas the real comfort of a car is measured by the ease with which it can be parked.

ARISTOGAMUS And what if someone has to make a journey with all his family?

SOCRATES In the first place he should ask himself if this wretched journey is really necessary; then, if the answer is affirmative, he can travel by train or aeroplane with the money he saved by buying a smaller car.

ARISTOGAMUS I fear, O Socrates, that you would soon bring about the collapse of the automobile industry.

SOCRATES Two: The top speed of a car should never exceed sixty kilometres an hour.[1] In the present day and age cars are being built with a top speed of over two hundred kilometres per hour. There is one thing I should dearly like to ask the manufacturers and the competent authorities: given that the laws of the country prohibit speeds in excess of 140 kilometres per hour even on the motorways, where on this earth can cars make full use of all that power?

ARISTOGAMUS The law forbids the effective, not the potential speed of a car.

SOCRATES You know my attitude to the Laws. If I were travelling on the Athens to Marathon motorway one day at two hundred kilometres an hour and the Law overtook me and, having stopped me, were to say: 'O Socrates, what were you thinking of, travelling at that speed? Do you not realize that by exceeding the speed limit you are destroying us, and that in destroying us you destroy the whole nation? Do you not know that eight thousand people are killed in road accidents every year in this country alone? Can you tell us what you will do in those seven minutes you saved by travelling at two hundred kilometres an hour?' Just suppose that happened, Aristogamus, how would we answer these and other similar questions?

ARISTOGAMUS You, O Socrates, always reason in utilitarian terms and underestimate the pleasure of having something in hand, the thrill of speed, the excitement of pushing something to the limits, the purity of aerodynamic lines. The vehicle you are dreaming about is a cart drawn by a donkey.

SOCRATES Not quite. I'll try to describe it for you. The car I have in mind, which is lodged in the World of Ideas formulated by my pupil Plato, is surrounded on

[1] 37.28 miles an hour.

all sides by a tough rubber bumper twenty centimetres high and of a similar thickness.

ARISTOGAMUS But the car you describe already exists in reality and can be found in any fairground as a 'bumper-car'! People would feel ashamed to be seen around in a car like that!

SOCRATES But in compensation the temper of drivers would be vastly improved. At present, every face you see behind the wheel of a car stuck in a traffic jam looks bitter and twisted. People are so frightened of touching or being touched by the vehicle nearest them that all other drivers become so many enemies against whom they must defend themselves. If my wrap-around rubber bumper were used, however, crash repair companies would go out of business and insurance costs would go down. People might actually start to enjoy nudging each other while they wait at the traffic lights. But see, here comes Meneandrus in his car.

PHAEDRUS Ah, Meneandrus, we were expecting you, and I, especially, am most curious about your car. Tell me all you can about this model so that I can form an opinion about it.

MENEANDRUS It's a Land-Rover, a four-wheel drive.

SOCRATES What does that mean?

MENEANDRUS It means that you can drive it comfortably even over rough ground.

SOCRATES Have you used it much so far on rough ground?

MENEANDRUS No, never.

SOCRATES Then why did you buy a four-wheel drive?

MENEANDRUS Because it looks much nicer than an ordinary car.

SOCRATES I don't think I shall ever understand today's youth. But I believe that Parmenides, as usual, will come to my aid.

MENEANDRUS I too, O Socrates, find it difficult to understand you. How does Parmenides come into the discussion?

SOCRATES Parmenides is a venerable Italian philosopher, my friend, who has a strange way of classifying human actions and every object he sees either as something that is or as something that is not. Well then, even without consulting him about this specific case, I am certain that were he with us now, he would classify your Land-Rover among the things that are not.

MENEANDRUS Are you joking? Tell Signor Parmenides that my Land-Rover is a car that most certainly is, since it cost me no less than four talents and has made me the envy of all the young men in Athens. And, if he still has any doubts, I'll take him for a spin outside the city and show him how well it takes corners and how easily I can push it up to 150 kilometres an hour.

SOCRATES I do not believe that Parmenides judges the quality of being by talents and much less by speed. Indeed, he would even deny that your car can be made to move at all. Parmenides denies the possibility of movement.

MENEANDRUS Your Parmenides must be mad. If you are truly his friend, take him to see Hippocrates to have his head examined.

SOCRATES The first question he would put to you, were it possible, would be this: 'What is a motor car?'

MENEANDRUS And I would reply: 'A car is a self-propelling means of transport with wheels and all the gadgets necessary for driving, such as a steering wheel, brakes, accelerator and so on.'

SOCRATES Very good. But even a humble Fiat 126 that costs but a few minae has all these things, or am I wrong?

ARISTOGAMUS You're quite right, Socrates.

SOCRATES So why has your friend Meneandrus expended four talents on a car which has exactly the same equipment as another car costing only a few minae?

MENEANDRUS But what line of reasoning is this, O Socrates! They're quite right when they call you 'the madman of Alopece'. Fancy comparing my Land-Rover with a Fiat 126! I might as well say that your Xanthippe and the goddess Aphrodite are the same woman just because they both have the same number of arms and legs! You are simply ignoring the lines, the comfort, and above all the prestige that a Land-Rover can confer on its owner.

SOCRATES Now you've fallen into the trap, my young friend. I was waiting for you like Orion lurking in the bushes by night waiting for the boar to appear at the drinking-hole. The drinking-hole in this case was the word 'prestige'. If I understand you aright, you believe that the sight of your Land-Rover must surely make all Athens gasp with admiration, so that one man says to another: 'Oh, what a beautiful car! I wonder who owns it?' and someone else says: 'Ah, the car belongs to Meneandrus, the magnificent and famous Meneandrus!' And thus the good qualities of the car are transferred to its owner. I therefore conclude that you have spent four talents in order to appear better, or to appear more worthy of the admiration of others.

MENEANDRUS So what's wrong about wanting the admiration of one's fellows?

SOCRATES Nothing, provided that the admiration is for yourself, but everything if the admiration is directed towards your car. I know that Aristippus has a car, too, and he's had a telephone installed in it...

MENEANDRUS Yes, he's got a Mercedes Turbo.

SOCRATES Now I find myself wondering what Aristippus will do with a telephone in his car, since he is a wastrel who does nothing and lives on unearned income.

MENEANDRUS I suppose he will use it to make telephone calls.

SOCRATES But is it essential that he does so while driving? Can he not, like all other mortals, stop the car for a minute and use a public telephone? Is Aristippus a stockbroker, a businessman, a doctor, to whom a few seconds' delay could have fatal results? The truth is that Aristippus' car phone is a substitute in the eyes of other people for qualities which he knows he does not possess. The question here is which is preferable, being or seeming, and it appears to me that Aristippus has opted for seeming.

MENEANDRUS I still don't understand what you are getting at, O Socrates. All I know is that I love this car more than anything else in the world.

SOCRATES And to think that Meletus is accusing me, publicly, of fabricating new Gods!

ARISTOGAMUS You, O Socrates, commit one grave error when you judge your fellow-beings. You think that every man should be for ever following some high ideal for which he should even be prepared to sacrifice his life. Well, let me tell you that there are plenty of simple people who would never harm anybody, who take life as it comes, living a day at a time and being satisfied with humble objectives. Does the fact that Meneandrus is infatuated with his car for the moment do you any harm?

SOCRATES It does no harm to me but it does a great deal of harm to him. The way of life you were describing is fairly common among men. The Turin school of philosophers has defined it as the 'theory of the weak-minded'. Those of Neapolis, who are less intellectual, for which they are severely criticized, have even put it into verse: *'Basta ca ce sta 'o sole / basta ca ce sta 'o mare / 'na nenna accore accore / e 'na canzone pe' cantà / chi 'a avuto, 'a avuto, 'a avuto / e chi 'a dato, 'a dato, 'a dato / scurdammoce 'o passato / simme è Napule paisà.*[2] Which doesn't alter the fact that a life spent in chasing inferior goals will be increasingly unhappy.

MENEANDRUS I'm perfectly happy with my Land-Rover.

SOCRATES Is it your first car?

MENEANDRUS No, I had a Porsche before.

SOCRATES And did you love the Porsche?

MENEANDRUS Yes, I did.

SOCRATES Then why did you change it for a Land-Rover?

MENEANDRUS What a question! Because the Land-Rover's a better car.

SOCRATES Before the Porsche, did you have another car?

MENEANDRUS Yes, a BMW. But why do you keep asking me these rambling questions?

SOCRATES Because I believe that a man who keeps to a single car, even if it's only a little runabout, is happier than a man possessed by a Daemon that forces him to change it every other day. You have not noticed, Meneandrus, that you are pouring wine into a jug with a hole at the bottom. You pour and pour but you will never be able to drink. Now that you have finally got your new car, don't you feel a kind of emptiness inside?

MENEANDRUS Do you really believe that owning nothing flashier than a 126 would make me happy?

SOCRATES To drink, we need no more than a small cup or even the hollow of our hand.

---

2 'All one needs is to be out in the sunshine and near the sea with a pretty girl beside one and a song to sing. What is done is done, what is over is over. For us, the people of Naples, the past is past.

PHAEDRUS From what you have said, O Socrates, I understand that I should give up the idea of buying a car because once this desire has been satisfied it will be followed immediately by another, even more costly one.

SOCRATES The need for possessions never relents once it has taken hold. But in spite of that, O Phaedrus, you may still buy your car; the important thing is that you do not become a slave to it. But know this, that it will not be in a car that you make the most important journey of your life, the one that takes you from where you are now into the depths of your own being.

# San Gennaro's Last Miracle

Two years of living in Naples and associating with Bellavista had completely transformed Cazzaniga. Apart from an 'e' that remained fractionally too open for a native of the south, he could almost have passed for a middle-class Neapolitan of the kind you expect to see, every Sunday morning, buying pastries from Pintauro on the way to Mass at Santa Caterina. The old Doctor Cazzaniga was now only a memory, while the new one never passed up the opportunity of chatting with Salvatore, discussing Inter and Napoli with Saverio, and grumbling about the traffic situation with whoever happened to be within earshot. And never in his life had he enjoyed himself more than in the porter's lodge. Every evening when he got back from his office, instead of going straight up to his flat he would use the entryphone to tell his wife that he had arrived and then drop into the porter's lodge for a social half hour with the Professor.

'What are you discussing?' asked Cazzaniga.

'Miracles,' replied Saverio.

'Miracles?' echoed Cazzaniga with an enquiring glance at Bellavista.

'Yes, miracles,' confirmed the Professor. 'Doctor, have you ever seen the miracle of San Gennaro from close to?'

'No. Why, is that possible?'

'Certainly. The Saint liquefies his blood twice a year, on 19 September and on the first Saturday in May, and he is nearly always punctual. Which is more than can be said for the Naples–Milan express.'

Cazzaniga was puzzled; he suspected he was having his leg

pulled. Then he plucked up courage and asked:

'And what does the Church have to say about it?'

'The Church, being prudent, equivocates,' replied Bellavista. 'The See of Naples believes in the miracle, the See of Rome is not quite so sure.'

'Did a saint called San Gennaro ever really exist?'

'Indeed he did. Furthermore he was an aristocrat, a scion of the great Roman family of the Januarii.'

'Am I right in thinking he was beheaded?' asked Cazzaniga.

'He was subjected to various tortures,' replied the Professor, 'including fire, the spiked girdle and *ad bestias*, and in the end he was beheaded. The sources are not all in complete agreement on the subject. All we know for sure is that he was put to death in 305 AD. At the time, San Gennaro was a young bishop in Benevento. One day, just as he had finished celebrating Mass, the news was brought to him that his colleague Sossio, Bishop of Nola, had been imprisoned and tortured. He was very happy to hear this and immediately decided to go with two of his subordinates, the deacon Festus and the lector Desiderius, to visit him in prison. It goes without saying that as soon as the Roman soldiers saw them arrive in Nola they cast all three into prison without further ado.'

'Professor, when you were talking about the arrest of Sossio, you said that San Gennaro was "very happy to hear this". Forgive my asking, but what did you mean?' asked Cazzaniga, very puzzled.

'And I repeat, he was very happy. The precise phrase used in the *Acts of Bologna* is: "He rejoiced at the news and hastened to bring him comfort." But to understand the significance of these words, you need to know what was going on in the fourth century AD. First and foremost, it was the great age of martyrs. In 303, the Edict of Diocletian began the Great Persecution. In Nicomedia alone, the emperor's elected capital, twenty thousand Christians were slaughtered. Almost half a million in Egypt. In Phrygia, one town was surrounded and burnt to the ground with all its inhabitants, Christian and non-Christian. In Lutetia Parisorum, which we know today as Paris, an entire hill was soaked with the blood of the Christian followers of the bishop Dionysius, later known as St Denis. Today this hill is called Montmartre, meaning 'Hill of the Martyrs'. The terms of Diocletian's edict prescribed that executions should be carried out with the maximum cruelty. One clause stated that, 'In cases where the torturer is judged to have been too lenient, he shall himself be subjected to torture.'

'*Mamma d'o Carmene!*'[1] breathed Saverio. 'Those ancient Romans were a right load of bastards!'

'Yes, and the Christians' response was even more radical. In effect, they turned to their torturers and said: "So you want to torture us? Splendid! But do us a favour and prolong the torture as much as you possibly can!" Christian sects arose dedicated to the sole aim of martyrdom. St Simeon Stylites was a case in point. Originally, he founded a sect whose name, literally translated, meant "those who do not sleep". They were a little group of believers who had decided to pass their lives in continual prayer, for which they were even prepared to go without sleep.'

'How on earth did they manage that?' asked Salvatore.

'As soon as one of them nodded off, the one next to him would shake him awake so that he could resume his prayers, and so they would go on until they all collapsed simultaneously. But then the first one who managed to wake up went and woke up all his colleagues and the praying started again. Simeon's companions finally threw him out for applying the rule too intransigently.'

'If you ask me,' said Salvatore, 'someone should have told him: "Simeò, get stuffed! Let's get some sleep!"'

'So then Simeon went and sat on a column ten metres high where he stayed, praying, for thirty years.'

'How did he manage for food?'

'He had a basket on a string . . .'

'A lunch-basket?'

'Yes. He let it down and hoped that passers-by would be generous.'

---

[1] *Madonna del Carmine*: a Neapolitan expression denoting extreme surprise. *Translator's note.*

'You certainly couldn't do such a thing nowadays,' commented Saverio. 'Just imagine, if I decided to become Saverio Stylites and went to sit on the War Memorial in Piazza Vittoria, the fire brigade would be along in ten minutes flat to order me down.'

'Professor,' asked Luigino, 'what does *ad bestias* mean?'

'It means "exposed to the beasts". In this instance, four Christians, Gennaro, Sossio, Festus and Desiderius, were fed to the bears in the Pozzuoli amphitheatre. But the bears laid themselves at the feet of San Gennaro like puppy-dogs and five thousand inhabitants of Pozzuoli were converted to the Christian religion. Timotheus, the Roman governor of the province, was so put out because the show had been spoilt that he condemned the four martyrs to a more definitive demise: decapitation. And while he was about it, he had three of the spectators decapitated at the same time for daring to protest. Nowadays the miracle happens in three separate places at the same time: in Naples, where the blood liquefies, in Pozzuoli, where the block where the saint was beheaded turns red, and in the home of Francesco Caravita, Prince of Sirignano, on whose neck a thin red line appears twice a year.'

'How does one get to see the miracle?' asked Cazzaniga.

'Nothing could be easier,' replied Bellavista. 'Next Saturday is the first Saturday in May. A procession leaves the Cathedral with the statue of the Saint at around five o'clock in the afternoon and proceeds by way of Spaccanapoli to the church of Santa Chiara where the miracle takes place.'

'Unfortunately,' sighed Doctor Cazzaniga, 'I'm due in Milan on Saturday evening.'

'What time's the flight?' asked Salvatore.

'Nine o'clock.'

'So there's no problem,' Salvatore reassured him. 'If San Gennaro knows you've got a plane to catch, he'll perform the miracle on the dot. Then we'll drive you to Capodichino.'

The following Saturday, the first in May and therefore the day of the miracle, found Bellavista and Salvatore waiting on the pavement outside the flats for Cazzaniga to appear. Salvatore, either out of respect for the Saint or mindful of the fact that he was to accompany the Professor to the airport later on, was wearing a jacket and tie.

'If he doesn't come soon,' sighed the assistant-deputy porter, 'he'll miss both the miracle and his flight to Milan.'

'What time does the procession start?' asked the Professor.

'It leaves the Cathedral at five. I would think it'll arrive at Santa Chiara by six-thirty at the latest. But remember, our friend then has to get to Capodichino.'

'And what time is it now?'

'Ten to five, and today being Saturday it'll take us at least half an hour to get to Spaccanapoli.'

'Here he comes,' exclaimed Bellavista as he turned to greet his friend.

'I'll only be in Milan for one day,' began Cazzaniga as he arrived, still slightly breathless and grasping a small overnight case. 'I've got a meeting in the morning at half past eight. More to the point, what time does the miracle take place?'

'They're only waiting till you turn up,' quipped Salvatore.

The three climbed into the car and the Professor headed out into the busy stream of traffic.

'Naples, Dottò, has always remained a pagan city,' said Bellavista as he let in the clutch. 'If there's one thing lacking in the religious make-up of my fellow-citizens, it's the concept of God.'

'You mean they're not monotheists.'

'Exactly. Neapolitans,' he continued, 'have always been slightly wary about God. You hardly ever hear a Neapolitan exclaim "My God!" like Protestants do. Our requests for help tend to be rather less direct, usually aimed at saints with a good track record preferably for dispensing the particular kind of assistance required. At the most, we'll apply to the Madonna with a simple "*Madonna mia, aiutaci tu!*"'

'Indeed, you Neapolitans – thanks to your Madonna of the Rosary at Pompeii – have always had a very strong Marian tradition.'

'Yes, but that isn't the point,' insisted the Professor. 'The fact is that the Person of the Madonna, seen as the Mother of Mercy, appeals to a population for whom forgiveness is a daily requirement. You see, Doctor, the factor that distinguishes Christianity from all other religions is precisely the role it assigns to the Madonna. Where practicalities are concerned, Christian morality is not very different from Buddhism. You find injunctions such as "love thy neighbour as thyself" in all faiths, and the concept of divine punishment is ubiquitous. It's the idea of forgiveness that is original. A Neapolitan poet, Ferdinando Russo, once wrote a poem about the Madonna in which God orders a little angel to be put in prison for some sin or other. Saint Peter tries in vain to make the Lord change his mind, but the only answer he gets is, "No, he's to stay there for a day and a night. I give the orders in Paradise." The little angel in his dark cell weeps, flaps his wings and cries aloud in fear. But when everyone else is sound asleep, the Madonna creeps along to his cell surreptitiously and gives him some tangerines.'

'That's probably why Neapolitans prefer to pray to the Madonna,' commented Cazzaniga. 'She represents the mother they remember from babyhood.'

'Sometimes,' said Salvatore, 'we pray to the souls in Purgatory, too.'

'Why not the souls in Paradise?' objected Cazzaniga. 'Surely they have better contacts than those in Purgatory.'

'Yes, but they don't give a brass monkey about us,' replied Salvatore. 'You see, Doctor, the souls in Paradise are above the fray; they live in a state of blessed ecstasy and nothing that happens on earth affects them in the slightest. But the souls in Purgatory are still suffering and need the prayers of their relatives to shorten the time of waiting. And this gives rise to a system of mutual assistance, so to speak, between those above and those below: we pray for them, asking for their punishment to be reduced, and they pray for us, helping us to land a job with the Council or win a prize in the Lottery.'

*

## 68 *The Dialogues*

By the time our three friends arrived in Spaccanapoli, the procession had already moved off. Turning out of a street at the top of Monte di Pietà, they met it at about the half-way mark.

'That's St Emiddio,' said Salvatore, pointing to the statue passing at that moment. 'If we hurry we can still reach the head of the procession. St Emiddio comes about number five or six in the order.'

'There was a time,' said Bellavista, 'when a saint's position in the procession depended on the number of favours he had granted throughout the year. The priests used to go around gathering information from the people and then compile a kind of classification, a Hit Parade of saintliness. But nowadays the court of San Gennaro has been reduced to about fifty saints, each represented in the procession by a silver statue.'

'So the one who comes last is a saint who doesn't work miracles?' asked Cazzaniga.

'The system no longer applies, but they say that the saint who brought up the rear during the last century was always a certain St Cosimo of Aversa. There's a legend about him concerning a peasant who owned a pear tree that never produced any pears. After a couple of years he decided to cut the tree down and sell it to a wood-carver who used it, of course, for a statue of St Cosimo. All the people of Aversa went to the church to ask favours of St Cosimo except our peasant. "*Te cunosco piro*," he said, meaning: "I knew you when you were a pear tree. If you couldn't produce any pears then, there's a fat chance of your answering prayers now!"'

With Salvatore acting as outrider, Bellavista and Cazzaniga made their way towards the head of the procession as fast as circumstances permitted. Every statue that passed found the Professor ready with a story to tell.

'That's St Alfonso Maria de' Liguori, a Neapolitan saint with a big following in the area around the Law Courts. Saint Alfonso looks after all those who have anything to do with the law. He was an advocate at the age of seventeen and, thanks to his silver-tongued oratory, won all his cases. But one day, just as he finished his summing-up, his client had an attack of conscience and admitted he was guilty. St Alfonso was so upset that he resigned on the spot. The incident had shown him that the only perfect justice was divine justice.'

'St Alfonso gets me out of paying parking tickets,' announced Salvatore.

'This is St Gaetano,' continued the Professor, 'a saint who never had much success around these parts. The Pope sent him to Naples as a missionary, but the Neapolitans sent him back to Venice. As a priest he was too self-effacing, too shabbily dressed, not at all what the people of those days were used to. Don't forget that this was the High Renaissance. The saint's reaction was to say, "Never mind, God is in Venice just as much as in Naples."'

'And who's this?' asked Cazzaniga as another statue passed by.

'That's St Crispin,' replied Bellavista. 'He and his brother Crispinian are regarded as the patron saints of shoemakers. Crispin and Crispinian fled from Rome following the Edict of Diocletian and settled in France, at a place called Soissons where, so it's said, they repaired shoes free for anyone who became converted to Christianity. However, things didn't work out too well for them there, either. They were caught by the Roman soldiers and beheaded in the market place. I believe their remains are now in Paris, in the church of Notre-Dame.'

'Does their blood liquefy, too?' asked Cazzaniga, no longer surprised at anything.

'Indeed not. There are only eleven saints in the whole world whose blood liquefies, and ten of them are in Naples.'

'Who is the eleventh?'

'That's St Pantaleone, whose blood liquefies in a village a few kilometres outside Naples.'

This concentration of miracles in and around Naples made Cazzaniga chuckle despite himself. Then he asked Bellavista: 'Don't you ever wonder, Professor, whether your fellow-citizens are maybe a mite gullible?'

'Because they believe in San Gennaro?' asked Bellavista. 'Well, they probably *are* slightly naïve, but no more credulous than most people in this country. Have you noticed that nowadays most Italians swear by the signs of the Zodiac? Even some of the most staid of our state organizations, such as the Post Office and television news programmes, put out daily horoscopes as if they were articles of faith. So, I ask myself, is a Neapolitan who believes in San Gennaro because he has seen with his own eyes the blood of the martyr liquefy in the phial any more ingenuous than the average Italian who believes he will meet his Great Love next week because Venus is about to enter the sign of Libra and because he was born at nine in the morning rather than at twelve?'

The Professor was interrupted by a sudden outburst of clapping as the silver statue of St Anthony Abbot passed by.

'Don't be misled by that enthusiasm,' said Bellavista to Cazzaniga. 'It's partisan. That's a group from Borgo Sant' Antonio Abate applauding their own patron saint. There are still people in Naples who don't accept San Gennaro as patron saint. It's an old story, going back to '99, the year of the Jacobin revolution. When the French arrived in Naples, San Gennaro refused to perform his miracle, almost as if he were protesting against the ousting of the Bourbons. So General Championnet, fearing a popular uprising, marched into the cathedral and pointed a pistol at the cardinal who had the phials in his hands. No one knows exactly what happened next. Maybe the cardinal's hands were shaking with fright, or maybe San Gennaro himself intervened to save his life, but anyway, the blood liquefied within seconds. The people, who had never understood the stance taken by the intellectuals and who were royalist to a man, were furious with San Gennaro for performing the miracle, and as soon as the French had gone they demoted him and replaced him with his direct rival, Sant'Antonio. Benedetto Croce reported that a shop in Rua Catalona displayed a painting for a time showing Sant'Antonio Abate belabouring San Gennaro.'

'Was Sant'Antonio also a Neapolitan saint?'

'Indeed not. He never left Africa,' replied the Professor emphatically. 'Sant'Antonio Abate, also called "the Great" to distinguish him from his Paduan namesake...'

'... who was small,' put in Salvatore.

'... was born in Egypt in the middle of the third century. When he was twenty he felt that his vocation lay in a life of asceticism, so he gave all his possessions to the poor and went to live in a ransacked tomb in the Valley of the Kings.'

'Forgive me for interrupting, Professor,' said Salvatore, 'but there haven't been any new saints for quite a long time now, have there?'

'Well, the process of canonization is a very long one.'

'But what I meant,' explained Salvatore, 'was that I can't remember a single case of someone in Naples giving away all his possessions to the poor for the sake of being made a saint.'

'You were telling me about Sant'Antonio,' said Cazzaniga to Bellavista, giving Salvatore a reproving look.

'As I was saying, Sant'Antonio shut himself up in an empty tomb until, deciding that this dwelling was too luxurious for an ascetic like himself, he took himself off into the desert and remained there, praying, until he was a hundred. How he managed to survive for so long no one will ever know. The saint's fame rests on his celebrated fights with the devil. He was tempted in every possible way, by hunger, thirst and sex. Apparently, while he was praying, two extraordinarily beautiful naked women crept out from under the mat he was kneeling on. The legend says that time and again he nearly yielded to temptation but always managed to defeat the devil in the end, and that when he was dying he said to Christ: "Where were you when I was wrestling with Satan?", and that Christ replied: "I was there right beside you, Antonio, but I wanted to see you win by your own unaided efforts."'

'Odd how the Neapolitans should have conceived such an affection for an unsociable hermit like Sant'Antonio,' mused Cazzaniga. 'Had he lived in Naples it would have been understandable, but if he never set foot outside Africa, then I just can't see ...'

'In fact, Naples has often taken a foreign saint to its heart,' Bellavista went on. 'Take the case of San Vincenzo Ferreri, the so-called "monacone". San Vincenzo lived in Spain and never came to Naples, and yet in the Sanità, one of the most typically Neapolitan quarters of the town, he is held in greater esteem than San Gennaro and Sant'Antonio rolled into one. San Vincenzo was a Dominican preacher, perhaps the greatest the church has ever known. The churches themselves were not big enough to hold all the people who wanted to hear him preach, so the poor man was obliged to deliver his sermons in the open air, standing in the middle of vast public squares. If you're wondering how he ever managed to make himself heard without the help of a microphone, the answer is that he used the wind to carry his voice as far as possible. And the people could tell in which direction the wind was blowing because they always put a pole with a streamer on it beside him.'

'Why do the Neapolitans love him so much?'

'Because he had no faith in the medical profession. One story describes how a doctor came to see him when he was apparently on his death bed, and he drove him out of the house with the words: "A man whose heart is set upon God has no need of medicine." The following day he was completely cured. Nowadays mothers in Sanità rely on him to look after the health of their children, and when a child recovers from some illness, the mother will dress him up as a monk and present him to San Vincenzo on his feast day.'

'And does it work?' asked Cazzaniga.

'Better than the USL[2],' replied Salvatore.

As soon as they were inside the church, Bellavista realized that there was a distinct possibility that Cazzaniga would be unable to see anything that day. The central nave was by now packed solid with people, and the side chapels were completely occupied by delegations representing the saints of the 'Court of San Gennaro'. The Professor, however, not one to be discouraged by such trifles, immediately decided to outflank the enemy.

'We must try another route,' he said to Cazzaniga. 'If we enter by the Majolica Cloister, we can cut through the Coro delle

---

[2] The Italian equivalent of the National Health Service.

Clarisse and come out right behind the altar.'

'Will they let us through?' asked Cazzaniga, not unreasonably apprehensive.

'In Naples you can always find some saint, relative or friend to get you, by hook or by crook, where you want to be,' replied Bellavista.

Setting off at a brisk pace, the Professor led his friends round to the back of the monastery where, on reaching an ancient door, he pressed the bell beside it without hesitation.

'We are friends of the Imperiali family,' he said to the monk who opened the door, 'and would like to be shown to a position near the altar.'

The monk shot him a keen glance, as if assessing the man before him rather than the plausibility of the connection claimed, then disappeared muttering an almost inaudible 'wait here'.

'Where does the Imperiali family come into the calculations?' asked Cazzaniga, anxious to glean every scrap of information connected with the miracle.

'It's one of the ten noble families that make up the Royal Treasury Committee,' replied the Professor. 'By ancient royal decree, every public manifestation concerned with the cult of the saint is entrusted to twelve representatives of the Benches, ten from the aristocracy and two from the commoners. I happen to know the Imperiali of Francavilla: extremely pleasant and very nice people.'

Meanwhile, Cazzaniga glanced at the outside of the monastery.

'This is a very beautiful church. The style is one of extreme, one might almost say stark, simplicity.'

'Indeed!' replied Bellavista with enthusiasm. 'It is the most typically Franciscan and, perhaps for that very reason, the most beautiful of all Italian churches. Robert of Anjou built it in the fourteenth century as a burial place for his family. Even then, it must have been just as bare and uncluttered. I once read that when the king's son, the young and very refined Prince Carlo, first saw the church, he told his father that the main body of the church looked like a stable and the transepts like so many mangers. And the king replied: "You just watch out, young man, that you're not the first who has to dine in one of those chapels!"'

Just then the monk returned and said, with the same detachment as before:

"Come with me.'

'Tell me,' asked Cazzaniga, walking beside him, 'off the record of course. In your opinion is this a real miracle?'

'It happens,' replied the monk.

The cardinal raised the casket above his head and showed the phials containing the still-congealed blood to the people. Inside the casket, a kind of round silver box protected by double layers of glass, were two small bottles, one larger than the other. The larger one was three-quarters filled with a dark brown substance. 'At first sight,' thought Cazzaniga, 'it looks like coffee.' The monk had placed Bellavista and his friends on the right of the altar, behind a group of kneeling nuns.

'You are all here to witness the miracle of the liquefaction of the blood,' said the cardinal, addressing the crowd. 'But I should like to put a question to you. Have you come to see a show, or truly to partake in a holy mystery? Because if your interest has been aroused merely by the paranormal phenomenon, then, I regret to say, you could as well have stayed at home. Your souls will not be saved by the dissolving of these few grammes of blood, but only by the dissolving of the selfishness in the depths of your heart. That is why I now invite you to concentrate on your prayers and to pray, all together: "I believe in God, the Father Almighty, . . .".'

'Professor,' whispered Salvatore, 'I'm afraid it looks as if it's going to be a lengthy affair today. The blood has usually liquefied by now.'

Doctor Cazzaniga started to worry about his plane. He glanced at his watch.

'If nothing happens within thirty minutes, I shall go and find a taxi.'

'No way, Doctor!' exclaimed Salvatore. 'Miracle or no miracle, we're taking you to Capodichino.'

'I've got my own theory about the miracle of San Gennaro,' murmured Bellavista.

'What is it?' asked Cazzaniga.

'As you probably know, the blood of the saint has been tested in every conceivable way, or rather every way possible without actually breaking the phials. Spectroscopic analysis carried out by Professor Lambertini, Professor of Anatomy at the University of Naples, proved it is indeed human blood. But in spite of that, the most fantastic hypotheses have been put forward by those wanting to denigrate the miracle. They have suggested that the blood liquefies in the warmth of the cardinal's hand, or even the warmth of the candles; others insist that it's a mixture of soap and ammonia or a paste concocted from gelatine and cinnabar ... in short, everyone has had their own pet theory, even chocolate has had its supporters...'

The cardinal, becoming aware of the whispering on his right, shot a reproving glance at Bellavista. The blood in the phial was still as hard as rock, and, to all appearances, just as unlikely to move. The cardinal raised the casket above his head again and by tilting it to one side showed that no liquefaction had as yet occurred.

'Some people think of this place as a theatre,' the cardinal thundered, 'and forget, or pretend to forget, that the Church was created by the blood of its martyrs. It's easy today to confess the faith of Christ. In San Gennaro's time it was much more difficult. But remember: it's one thing to declare oneself a Christian but it's quite another to live a Christian life...'

'What did the supporters of the chocolate theory have to say?' asked Cazzaniga, lowering his voice as much as possible.

'They suggested that the phials contain a mixture of chocolate powder, water, sugar, casein, whey and cooking salt. This mixture was actually prepared by a certain Albini, a Professor from the University of Naples, towards the end of the last century, and, to tell the truth, this illustrious chemist did manage to concoct something that looked solid on the outside and dissolved immediately when shaken. The main objection to Albini's theory was that in the fifteenth century, when the miracle of San

Gennaro first occurred, chocolate had not yet been imported from America.'

'And what is your own theory?'

'I should like to carry out an experiment that no one has yet attempted.'

'What's that?'

'To take some blood from any ordinary person, allow it to coagulate and then expose it to the crowd in a casket just like the one containing the blood of San Gennaro.'

'Then you think it's the Neapolitans' psychic energy that causes the liquefaction?'

'Exactly. I am convinced that three thousand ordinary Neapolitans, all concentrating upon the same phenomenon, can cause an alteration in a material substance.'

'And what about three thousand Milanese?'

'They'd never do it in a million years,' replied Bellavista with conviction. 'They are too rationally minded.'

'Professor,' said Salvatore, intervening, 'I may be wrong but I reckon that there are people who can perform small miracles and people who can't. If there is one single person here who has the gift, the miracle's in the bag, as it were. Shall I tell you, for instance, who could perform really great miracles if he wanted to?'

'Who?'

'Maradona.'

'Maradona indeed!' exclaimed Cazzaniga with a very slightly contemptuous glance at Salvatore.

'Absolutely, Doctor, Maradona,' repeated Salvatore. 'I've been putting him to the test for quite a time now. When I want something really important, I say to myself: "Maradona, come to my aid!" and I swear to you that nine times out of ten it works.'

'Salvatore!' protested Cazzaniga. 'Stop talking nonsense! We're in church.'

'But think, Doctor. Not even our Lord Jesus Christ knew that he could work miracles until he tried it.'

'According to the Gospel of St John, he did,' said Bellavista. 'When the wine ran out at the marriage in Cana, Mary begged him to perform a miracle and he refused, saying, "My time is not yet come", and he was right. It would have been wrong to start with a miracle like that...'

A deep murmuring ran all round the church, immediately followed by prolonged applause. The blood had liquefied. The cardinal raised the casket as high as possible and, as he tilted it onto its side, the blood washed around in the phials. The Gentleman of the Handkerchief, one of the Deacons of the Royal Committee, waved the precious embroidered handkerchief in the air to indicate to the faithful at the back of the church that San Gennaro had worked the miracle. All those around the altar knelt before the sacred relic and Bellavista and Cazzaniga could do no less than kneel with them and await their turn to kiss the casket. Cazzaniga was considerably shaken. Until the day before, the miracle of San Gennaro had been no more than a popular myth. Now he was no longer sure what it was. He had seen the liquefaction take place before his very eyes, at a distance of no more than five metres. But was it genuine? Who could tell! Perhaps the monk who had led them to their place beside the altar had the right idea: 'It happens'.

After half past eight in the evening, Naples' airport, Capodichino, suddenly becomes deserted. The flight for Venice has already left and the only one still showing on the flight departure boards is the nine o'clock for Milan. The bar is shut, so is the newspaper kiosk, the rows of taxis at the main door have dispersed and even the colourful throng of peripatetic vendors that usually crowds the central hall has melted away. No one is trying to flog watches, porn videos or cigarette lighters, no wide boys with shifty expressions are circulating with offers of dubious services.

Shortly after Bellavista, Salvatore and Doctor Cazzaniga arrived at the airport, the loudspeakers announced that the flight for Milan was delayed. There was, however, no indication of the length of the delay. Despite Cazzaniga's repeated suggestions that they should return home, Bellavista and Salvatore decided to stay until his flight left.

'Our pleasure, Doctor,' said Salvatore. 'Besides, I've only ever been in an aeroplane once in my life, when I went to see Napoli playing somewhere in Russia. Tirbisi ... Tiblisi ... Tiribisi ... Something like that. I must admit that before take-off I was shivering in my shoes. An aeroplane, I told myself, is always an aeroplane, it's up in the sky, and you can't say stop I want to get off. So when the time came, I got into such a panic just as I was about to climb the steps that my friends had to carry me bodily to my seat and strap me into it. Anyway, after we had been flying for about an hour, and I was beginning to get used to it, I saw someone walking down the aisle. Hallo, I thought, so one can actually get up and walk about, and I asked the person sitting next to me where the chap was going. He said: He's probably going to the toilet. Going to the toilet? I said. Do you mean one can actually go to the toilet up here? Yes, he said. So then I said: you make yourself comfortable and then where the stuff lands it lands. No, he said, nothing lands anywhere: it all stays on board because otherwise we wouldn't be very popular, especially when flying over a foreign country. Anyway, I wanted to go to the toilet, and this you won't believe, Doctor, but I had hardly sat down when I heard the stewardess call out: "Attention, attention, we are now flying over the Alps." But I was already in such a state of nerves that as soon as I heard her say "Attention" the first time, I came flying out of the toilet without stopping to do up my trousers.'

Cazzaniga smiled at Salvatore's anecdote, then glanced towards the bar, saying:

'Aren't there any other bars in the airport?'

'No,' replied Salvatore, 'and it's a wonder they've even got this one.'

'As I was saying,' said Bellavista, as if he were summarizing an argument that had been interrupted only a minute ago, 'the Neapolitans are still pagan. They believe in specialized gods: they pray to Santa Lucia when they have problems with their sight, to San Pasquale Baylon, better known as "Bailonne", when they want to marry off a daughter, to San Ciro if they need a medical specialist and to San Cristoforo if they have to drive from Naples to Rome in a Fiat 500. Nothing has changed since the ancient

Greeks, two thousand years ago, worshipped either Artemis or Ares depending upon whether they were going out hunting or to war.'

'And what do you believe in?' asked Cazzaniga.

The Professor said nothing for a while. He seemed not to have heard the question. Then, slowly, he began to mutter.

'Well ... it's difficult to say, off the cuff ... Years ago I was attracted by the Arian heresy, concerning the humanity of Christ, and maybe that's the theory I still prefer. You could call me a "Christian atheist".'

'Does that mean atheist or Christian?' enquired the justifiably puzzled Salvatore.

'Atheist and Christian at the same time,' declared the Professor. 'Atheist because I cannot believe in the existence of God, and Christian because I try to follow the precepts of Christ who was, in my opinion, the most important man who was ever on this planet. Let's talk about God first. What do we mean by God? Hope in a life to come? In that case, I must make it clear that I have no interest in any theory of eternal bliss or of reincarnation unless it is connected in some way to the past. If all memory of a past life is expunged, what sense is there in talking about reincarnation? What's the use of knowing that I was Julius Caesar in another life if I cannot retain any memory of the experience? And as for some hypothetical future existence, as "pure spirit", how can I be expected to be enthusiastic about any kind of super-terrestrial life that denies me any contact with the people I love and who are still upon the earth? For me, "to live" means "to love those whom I love". The greatest defect of the Kingdom of Heaven is the absence of telephones. I could demonstrate the existence of God by purely dialectical means such as: "Does God exist?" "I don't know." "So you admit there is something beyond your comprehension?" "Yes." "Then be kind enough to call that something God." All right, but where does that kind of reasoning leave us? Is it really that important to know that God exists? Isn't it more important to know that Love exists? And the personification of Love is Jesus Christ.'

Salvatore, hearing the word Christ, shot a glance at Cazzaniga as if to say: now everything's clear.

'What was so revolutionary about the teaching of Christ?' continued Bellavista, who seemed determined not to allow any opposition. 'He said: "Turn the other cheek", and he said it at a time when a man's life was of less value than a goat's. Do you know the parable of the labourers in the vineyard, Doctor? No? Then I'll tell it to you ...'

'After all, we've got nothing else to do,' added Salvatore by way of encouragement.

'Matthew, chapter 20 verses 1 to 16,' the Professor announced. 'A householder asked some men to work in his vineyard. Some men arrived at the first hour, others at the third and some more at the sixth. The last men arrived at the eleventh hour, shortly before sunset. When the evening had come, the householder gave each of them a penny, the same amount to those who had worked all day as to those who had only been there for the last five minutes. What does the parable mean? According to Father Ferruccio, the priest of San Gioacchino, the penny represents Paradise, and the reward of Paradise is within the reach of everyone, even those who only repent in the last five minutes of their lives. That's all very well, but some people might object. We can imagine one of the men saying to another: "Hey, I got up at five o'clock in the morning to come to work and you arrived, fresh as a daisy, at six o'clock in the evening, and what happens at the end of the day? We both get paid exactly the same! Is that what you call Justice?" Oh yes, I reply, that's Justice, because the truth of the matter is that the penny paid by the owner of the vineyard is false coin, because Paradise does not exist, because the only real reward is having worked in the vineyard of the Lord. Someone who loves receives his reward straight away, because only through loving can he know the subtle beauty of love and friendship. It is in our own interests to be good.'

'Professor,' said Salvatore, 'when I listen to you I always think you are right, but when I go out into the street and mix with other people I see that what you've said doesn't really work. The truth of the matter is that if a man is kind and generous towards his neighbour, his neighbour just walks all over him. The first rule for survival in Naples is do the other man down as often as possible. You only get on by wheeling and dealing...'

'My dear Salvatore,' Bellavista interrupted, 'I regret to observe that all the time I spent explaining Parmenides to you was wasted.'

'Parmenides?' asked Salvatore with a puzzled frown. 'Who was Parmenides? I have to admit that I can't quite remember for the moment...'

'Parmenides, the theory of Being,' urged the Professor, trying to jog Salvatore's memory about a lesson delivered some time ago. 'My dear Salvatore, your neighbour can only cheat you out of your non-being, and non-being is something that should not concern you at all. What can your neighbour take from you? He may carry off your money, power or success ... but so what? Money, power and success are only appearances, and appearances are certainly not what you come into the world for. Whenever you meet someone, you have a clear choice: you can cheat him or make a friend of him, but you can't do both. So, in that moment when you find yourself faced with the choice between cheating a man and loving him, you can't help realizing that the warmth of an embrace is the only thing that can make you feel alive.'

The Professor's last words were drowned by the loudspeaker announcement of a further delay of the 9 p.m. flight. Cazzaniga looked at his watch again and muttered irritably:

'Good God! It's nearly ten o'clock. We're an hour late already, and now they're talking about yet another delay. If this goes on I shan't be in Milan until after midnight!'

'And we can't even get a drink!' added Bellavista.

'We could go outside and see if there's a bar open,' suggested Cazzaniga.

'What's the point?' Salvatore objected. 'There's nothing near the airport, and if we took the car we'd wind up in the thick of the traffic again.'

'This is simply not good enough,' burst out Bellavista, raising his voice. 'This business of the bar being closed makes me really angry. I find it totally unacceptable that the airport serving a metropolis like Naples should not have a single bar which stays open round the clock for the convenience of all the travelling public, day and night.'

'OK, Professor, but don't get so worked up. Accept the fact that the bar's closed and there's nothing we can do about it. Only a miracle by San Gennaro could make it reopen.'

The words were scarcely out of Salvatore's mouth when a middle-aged man came up to Bellavista and said:

'Excuse me, Doctor, but I happened to overhear you saying you were thirsty. If you come with me over to the bar, I could, as an exception, get you something to drink.'

The man then went to the bar, took a key from its hiding place behind a poster, opened the catch of a cold storage container and asked:

'What can I get you?'

'Let's see,' said Bellavista. 'I'll go for a beer. What would the rest of you like?'

'I'll have a beer, too,' said Salvatore.

'If there is one,' ventured Cazzaniga, 'I'd prefer a Coca-Cola.'

'So that's two beers, please, and one Coca-Cola,' said Bellavista.

The man peered into the container, took out a Coca-Cola and a suitable glass, then turned to the Professor, saying:

'Would one can of beer and two glasses be enough?'

'Yes, thank you,' replied the Professor.

The man poured out the beer and the Coca-Cola. As Salvatore put the glass to his lips, he found himself thinking that the man behind the bar bore a truly striking resemblance to San Gennaro: two peas in a pod! But what was so surprising about that? He had invoked the Saint, and although there had been no one anywhere near them at the time, this individual had suddenly materialized as if out of thin air.

'How much do I owe you?' asked Cazzaniga, forestalling the Professor.

'Nothing,' replied their unknown friend. 'I don't own the bar, I just happen to know where the keys are kept.'

# *The Day Before*

'If I could only clinch a few sales in Naples, Sicurat would open a small branch here, and within days I'd be sales manager for the whole central-south region.'

Giorgio Loffredo, Bellavista's son-in-law, had just come back from Milan. He had been working in the north of the country for two years now, and every time he set foot in Naples he was required to provide an update of his news to the entire staff of the porter's lodge, meaning to Donn'Armando, Don Ferdinando and Salvatore, respectively the porter, the assistant porter and the deputy-assistant porter of 58, Via Petrarca. The present conversation was taking place under the archway leading from the courtyard to the street.

'And would you return to Naples for good?' asked Salvatore.

'Of course I would, and that's why I'm so keen to find customers in Naples. Honestly, Salvatò, there's no way I can go on living in Milan. Patrizia, lucky girl, has got used to it. But she's young, she's made friends, she even speaks Milanese. Not me. Maybe I'm just not adaptable enough, but I shan't ever feel at home there. Shall I tell you what happened to me last week? There was this man, Gorini, living in the same block of flats and on the same floor as us; like me, he was a qualified architect, but he specialized in interior design. He must have been forty-five, forty-seven or thereabouts. We used to have a chat from time to time. You know how it is, you meet someone the first time in the lift, then you run into them in the bar the next morning and while you're waiting for a coffee you get talking. Wonderful weather, isn't it! Where do you work? I'm with Sicurat, a Swiss company. Oh really? I design interiors. Anyway, that was the way things were between us, just the occasional good morning and good evening, and then I didn't see him at all for a couple of months. I asked Signor Ernesto, the porter of the block, a nasty piece of work with a clipped moustache, what was going on, and he said: "Architect Gorini's dead." "Dead?" I said. "What did he die of?" "He's dead," he repeated, and walked off. "Here's a fine state of things," I said to myself. "How can a fellow die without letting anyone know?" It made me think. Do you know, I never saw the street door left ajar as a mark of respect, nor any funeral hangings, nor the coffin being carried downstairs, nor any sign of family mourning! And something else puzzled me: how did they keep it all so dark? Patrizia just shrugged and said it must have happened one weekend. But does it strike you as natural? When someone dies in Naples, ye gods, the whole street gets involved. Everyone knows how the person died and what of, fellow-tenants are there to comfort, friends come to the wake, a neighbour brings round hot drinks, and that's how friendships are made. And if that doesn't happen what's the good of dying in the first place?'

'Don't let it worry you too much,' commented Donn'Armando. 'Professor Bellavista's right when he says that we're two separate nations united by the same television programmes!'

'Tell me,' said Salvatore, 'how many do you have to sell to claim the right for you and your family to be transferred back to Naples?'

'Ten would be enough. That's the minimum to qualify for an office and a secretary.'

'Forgive me for butting in,' said a tall, thin man with the hollow cheeks of an Edoardo De Fillippis. 'My name's Scalese and I would like to ask you a question: you said . . .'

'This is my cousin Antonio,' Salvatore said, interrupting him. 'He's a knife-grinder who lost his home in the earthquake and has been living for the past four years in a container on the Overseas Exhibition site with a wife and three children.'

'As I was saying,' Scalese continued, 'I arrived late so I didn't hear what you were saying to begin with. But as I'm involved not only with grinding knives but also with the import-export business, there's something I wanted to ask you. If I understood you correctly, you represent a Swiss company.'

'Yes, Sicurat,' said Giorgio.

'And what do you sell?'

'Nuclear fall-out shelters.'

This information took the knife-grinder's breath away. After a few seconds, with no comment apparently forthcoming, Giorgio continued.

'Sicurat is the leading company in this field, with a 35 per cent share of the market. All industrialized countries are now equipping themselves. In Switzerland, 84 per cent now own a nuclear fall-out shelter. In Israel we've now touched the 99 per cent mark and in Sweden we've achieved 88 per cent.'

'My friend,' said Salvatore's cousin, interrupting again, 'I don't want to dampen your enthusiasm, but I'm afraid you'll have a hard time of it in Naples. People haven't got enough money even to carry on a normal, everyday life, so the thought of them laying out cash in order to go on living after a nuclear bomb's been dropped on them is so much pie in the sky!'

'You're not serious?!' exclaimed Giorgio, obviously well up in his subject. 'With those Nato bases on the doorstep, Naples is a Prime Risk Zone and all you can do is joke about it?! Don't you realize that the Russians have an SS20 missile with a three-stage nuclear warhead already aimed at Naples and that it would be the first to be launched?'

'See what a spot we're in,' sighed Salvatore, looking round at the others. 'As soon as war breaks out the Russians score three headers against us! I've always said that the sooner those Americans from Nato get out, the better. After all, they've never brought in any dollars. You may not have realized it, but they don't trust Neapolitan shopkeepers. My wife, Rachelina, used to work part-time for one of them and she told me that they even import their own toilet paper from America. The Russian secret service should know about this sort of thing and they ought to build a special missile with just one warhead, and aim it with great precision at the Nato base.'

'Sure,' commented Bellavista's son-in-law. 'The Russians are going to start making missiles to order now!'

'Say what you like,' continued Scalese sceptically, 'but in my opinion you'll never sell these shelters in Naples.'

'How do you know?' retorted Giorgio confidently. 'Apart from anything else, sooner or later there may well be a law to encourage people to build nuclear fall-out shelters.'

'What sort of a law would that be?' enquired Donn'Armando.

'One like they already have in Switzerland,' Giorgio replied. 'The state pays 50 per cent of the cost of nuclear defence measures. Say you live in Lugano and you've got a cellar you want to make proof against nuclear attack. Nothing easier. You simply show the plans to the local council and the state immediately chips in with half the necessary funding.'

'I can just imagine what would happen in Italy if we had a law like that!' exclaimed Salvatore, laughing. 'Every toilet that needed repairing would become a nuclear shelter!'

'I can only repeat myself,' Scalese continued doggedly, determined to maintain his role of defeatist to the bitter end. 'Don't delude yourself. The Italian exchequer hasn't got a lira to bless itself with, and I should know, being an earthquake victim and a hereditary one at that ...'

'Hereditary?' asked Giorgio, his interest aroused.

'Yes. My father and grandfather were earthquake victims before me. Casamicciola, 1883. Do you know what people call me? ... Mercalli.[1] Anyway, as I was saying, ever since the earthquake in November 1980 I have been living in a container on the Overseas Exhibition site. (Incidentally, when you do me the honour of paying me a visit, remember that my container is the thirteenth on the right if you come from Viale Kennedy: do drop in for a coffee sometime.) Do you know what's happening now? I'm in danger of losing even that shitty apology for a home. And why? Because the company that supplied the container says it hasn't had its money from the Council and is threatening to

---

[1] Mercalli: A scale for measuring earthquakes according to their perceptible effects. Called after the Italian seismologist G. Mercalli (1850–1914). *Translator's note.*

re-possess from one day to the next. So I ask you, is it likely that an authority that can't even guarantee a container to a second-generation earthquake victim four years after the event will be any more successful in building shelters for those people who want to go on living under the ground when everyone above it is dead?'

It was noon. Avvocato Capuozzo, landlord of the tiny flat occupied by two elderly spinsters, the Finizio sisters, was crossing the courtyard. It was the fourth of the month and Capuozzo knew from experience that if he relaxed his hold for a minute the sisters would spend all their pension money and he would have the devil's own job to get his hands on the few lire to which he was entitled under the fair rent act. There would be tears, curses and faked suicide attempts.

In one corner of the courtyard, Salvatore and the architect Giorgio Loffredo, Bellavista's son-in-law, were taking measurements. Salvatore was holding one end of a twenty-metre tape while the architect, at the other end, made chalk marks on the ground.

Noticing the activity, Capuozzo slackened his pace. He decided that, as one of the proprietors of the condominium, he was entitled to ask why those measurements were being taken.

'Salvatò,' asked Capuozzo, 'what's happened? More trouble with the drains? Has that elbow-joint come adrift yet again?'

Capuozzo was especially sensitive where the drains were concerned. Not a year went by without the sanitary arrangements of the building causing him some problem. There was, in particular, one bend directly under the waste-pipe leading from his flat that had been a continual thorn in his side. It kept getting blocked and every time he called in a plumber to clear it, it cost him a million lire. 'You think a million's nothing, don't you?' he would moan. 'Well, let me tell you that it is precisely my year's rent from the Finizio sisters. It doesn't worry them if the pipes burst. They just carry on paying their "fair rent" while I'm cast, by some people, in the role of the wicked capitalist exploiting the poor old dears. Just carry on voting Communist, go on! This is the sort of justice we have to put up with in Italy nowadays!'

'No, it's nothing to do with that, Avvocà,' said Salvatore. 'We're taking measurements for installing an underground nuclear fall-out shelter.'

'What do you mean, a nuclear fall-out shelter?'

'I'll explain, Avvocato,' said Giorgio, intervening with a smile as he rolled up the tape. 'I represent Sicurat of Lugano, Atomic Security. A Swiss company that manufactures nuclear fall-out shelters. Now, as the company is considering opening a branch in Naples, I've managed to persuade the Swiss directors to install the first shelter in Naples free of charge. It'll be a demonstration shelter, so to speak, a kind of shop window. So when I was asked to select a site for this first installation, I thought where better than our own building? The whole expense of the installation will be borne by Sicurat.'

'Yes, I understand that, young man,' replied Capuozzo, 'but you'll have to find out if all the proprietors are in agreement about any such plan. And then the drainage system is right down here, and the drainage system is problem-prone . . .'

'Avvocà,' interrupted Salvatore, 'perhaps you didn't quite understand. The Swiss are not only letting us have the shelter for free, they are also footing the bill for all the necessary digging, so we have a golden opportunity for re-paving the courtyard and having the drains put right.'

'Do whatever you like, Salvatò,' Capuozzo retorted irritably, 'but remember that where this courtyard is concerned no one's allowed to plant as much as a sprig of basil without the consent of the joint owners.'

Condominium Man (*homo condominus*), as we all know, is not a normal being but a kind of Dr Jekyll. Until five minutes prior to a committee meeting of the proprietors (the second meeting, naturally, since the first, for some obscure reason, is always considered formal) he may be generally regarded as a nice man, courteous, friendly, even generous at times, but as soon as he crosses the threshhold of the room where the meeting is to be held he is transformed into a hair-splitting Athenian Sophist, a nuisance-monger who, rather than yield on a matter of principle, will be quite prepared to start legal proceedings at the drop of a hat.

The condominium situated at No. 58, Via Petrarca was divided into three schools of thought, adhered to respectively by the owner-occupiers, the landlords of derestricted apartments, and the landlords of apartments subject to a fixed-rent agreement. Capuozzo, undisputed leader of the last-named faction, had always been a ferocious opponent of anyone who suggested even a minimal improvement, tirelessly dedicated to the task of ensuring that the lives of the fixed-rent tenants should remain as joyless as possible.

The most usual bone of contention was the heating system which Passalacqua, leader of the owner-occupiers, wanted to centralize and replace with a German system and which Capuozzo held to be completely superfluous in a city like Naples that, according to him, enjoyed an equatorial climate. 'And what do we do when it gets cold?' Passalacqua would shout. 'Put on a coat or go to bed,' his adversary replied waspishly. In fact there was only one central heating system that would meet with Capuozzo's approval: a Nazi-style gas oven.

The meeting we are concerned with had been summoned in support of Professor Bellavista's son-in-law, to discuss Sicurat's offer of installing a nuclear fall-out shelter. However, there were always committee members ready to ignore the agenda and seize the opportunity to air their pet grievances. This was no exception.

'The first thing we should do,' said Signora Sbordone Colajanni (owner-occupier) 'is discuss the possibility of doing away with the coin-box in the lift. That silly contraption causes nothing but problems. Fifty-lire pieces have now virtually disappeared, and every time someone resorts in desperation to using a metal button, the lift is put out of order for a week. And in the end what do we stand to gain? Scarcely ever more than a hundred thousand lire a month, which, split between twenty-four residents, is nothing at all. Even Dr Stoppetti complains about the coin-box. He says that Naples is the only place where you still find such mediaeval contraptions.'

'Oh dear, I'm sorry that Dr Stoppetti should have been driven to complain!' exclaimed Capuozzo with heavy irony. 'Of course we'll remove the coin-box at once for his convenience. Then no doubt his landlord, Cavaliere Improta, who I see is with us today, will reimburse the money we stand to lose.'

'I see,' retorted Improta acidly, 'you think I'm stupid enough to make a gift of a hundred thousand a month to the administration!'

'You'd hardly notice it,' snapped Capuozzo, 'seeing that you squeeze a million and a half every month out of Stoppetti!'

'Listen!' thundered Professor Bellavista. 'I usually steer clear of these residents' meetings because, in your capacity as residents, frankly you make me sick. The business before us today, however, interests me personally and I should like to discuss it. My son-in-law, as he has already stated, would like to install a nuclear fall-out shelter under the courtyard . . .'

'The truth, my dear fellow,' shouted Improta, getting to his feet and jabbing a finger in the direction of Capuozzo, 'is that you're jealous!'

'Jealous! Me?' replied Capuozzo, also rising from his seat. 'Hardly, my dear fellow: you're quite wrong there. I'm simply defending my own interests.'

'That's it: you're jealous,' repeated Improta. 'Jealous because two of my fixed-rent tenants died leaving the apartments derestricted, while your Finizio women are bursting with health and obviously have no intention of going to their Maker.'

'Can we please have an end to this bickering?' implored Bellavista. 'Could I ask you to postpone this debate on the health of your respective tenants for five minutes or so and turn the teeniest bit of your attention towards the matter of the nuclear fall-out shelter?'

'Professor,' retorted Capuozzo testily, 'the installation of the shelter has already been discussed and permission refused. The residents' committee will not allow the courtyard to be dug up despite the fact that your son-in-law's company is based in Switzerland and may be prepared to give every guarantee under the sun. And let's not forget that the drainage system is beneath the courtyard and you don't mess about with drains.'

'The trouble is, my dear Professor, that the shelter is too small,' objected Signora Sbordone Colajanni. 'If it were big enough for everyone, I could see the point of it. But as it stands, it's useless. Say one day an atomic bomb were to explode, what would happen? We'd end up as a pile of murdered corpses outside the shelter!'

'I see your point,' replied Bellavista. 'But apart from the fact that the shelter would be joint property which could be sold eventually to any one of the residents, the present situation is that my son-in-law needs to install it in order to demonstrate it to potential customers and attract orders from them. See it from my point of view. If the lad can establish himself in the area, he will be immediately transferred to Naples, and when he returns my daughter returns with him.'

A few seconds of silence underlined the realization that the discussion on the agenda had less to do with economics than with a father's sacrosanct desire for the return of a daughter condemned to live in Milan. It was Capuozzo himself who eventually broke the silence.

'Very well, Professor. I propose that the committee give its consent for the temporary erection of a nuclear fall-out shelter in the courtyard but above ground, not below. I suggest that we give your son-in-law special permission to exhibit for two months. If by the end of two months he has failed to make any impression, it means that Naples is not interested in the product.'

'And where are my tenants supposed to park?' protested Improta.

'On the street like everyone else,' replied Capuozzo, more waspish than ever. 'And I hope their cars get stolen!'

'Timidity belongs both to the world of Love and to the world of Liberty,' said Bellavista. 'It is the daughter of Love because there is a direct correlation between a person's timidity and their sensitivity and gentleness of character, but since it springs from the fear of invading another person's privacy, it is also the daughter of Liberty.'

On this Tuesday, as on every other, a philosophy lesson was in full swing at Professor Bellavista's residence. Those present were Salvatore, Saverio the street-sweeper, Colonel Santanna and the poet Luigino. The subject under discussion was timidity in Ancient Greece.

'Professor,' said Saverio, intervening, 'your son-in-law is too timid. In my opinion he's in the wrong job. He's just not a salesman. From the very start, the way he presents himself when he's trying to make an appointment is enough to stop you wanting to buy anything from him. Yesterday morning I went with him to Citalcon, a furriers in Casagiove. Well, believe me, the doorkeeper didn't even give him time to open his mouth; as soon as he clapped eyes on him he said, 'Sorry, we're not interested, our storerooms are full of the stuff.' And he slammed the door in his face. I had to intervene myself to get him an interview with the proprietor.'

'And then what happened? Did he persuade him to buy a shelter?' asked Salvatore.

'Anything but!' replied Saverio. 'The boss at Citalcon told him he was up to his ears in debt and if nuclear war broke out his one regret would be that he wouldn't survive long enough to see all his bills go up in smoke.'

'Timidity can, however, be overcome with practice,' continued Bellavista, turning a deaf ear to the comments about his son-in-law. 'Crates the Cynic used to go out every evening and insult the whores he found waiting at the crossroads round Athens. And he did this in order to train himself to deal with his opponents in the agora the following morning.'

'He must have been at the receiving end of some pretty ripe language, I would think!' chortled Saverio.

'He was once asked to help an extremely timid boy, Metrocles, whose parents were worried because he blushed every other minute like a shy girl. The parents thought that Crates the Cynic would be able to instil some virility into the lad and help him to confront the trials and tribulations of life with more confidence. The first thing Crates did was to take the boy to a gymnasium to toughen him up. He said that physical strength would give him a better sense of security. Unfortunately, right in the middle of a weight-lifting exercise, Metrocles broke wind...'

'You mean he farted?' asked Salvatore, afraid he had not heard aright.

'Yes, flatulence.'

'Was it audible or inaudible flatulence?'

'Audible.'

'And this is written down in the history of philosophy?' asked Salvatore dubiously.

'Indeed, Diogenes Laertius tells the story.'

'Good grief!'

'When Metrocles saw that everyone had stopped what they were doing and were looking around in puzzlement, he blushed and immediately decided to commit suicide...'

'That was rather an overreaction, wasn't it?' exclaimed Salvatore. 'Suicide, indeed! When something like that happens you apologize, you say, "Sorry, chaps, I've got a bit of flatulence," and everything's all right again. Otherwise, heaven only knows how often we ourselves would have been obliged to commit suicide!'

'All very well, Salvatò,' countered Saverio, 'but remember that the lad was timid anyway... and, to be honest, he had every reason to be embarrassed.'

'So Crates,' Bellavista said, pursuing his topic doggedly, 'took him aside and said: "Now, Metrocles, dear boy, you have said you wanted to kill yourself and if that's your decision I respect it. However, I should be happier if such a decision were the result of a deliberate choice. Do you know what death means? No? Death means annihilation. So before you commit suicide, I think you should compare annihilation with what you stand to gain if you decide to live. Tomorrow I'm going to introduce you to the highest authorities in the polis, so you will be able to judge what you could have done with your life."'

'Good old Crates!'

'The first thing the philosopher did the next day was to eat a couple of pounds of beans; then he took Metrocles by the arm and led him to the archons of Athens. Bowing to each one in turn, he told the lad: "These are the men who control the destiny of the polis." And meanwhile, he emitted an almighty fart...'

'He was suffering from flatulence?' enquired Salvatore, on whom the term had made a very deep impression from the start.

'Quite right. Then they went to the ten strategoi. "These," said Crates, "are the military commanders charged with the defence of Athens in time of war." And he farted again. In fact he did it so often that Metrocles came round to thinking that it was completely normal.'

'And you say this is all written down in the history of philosophy?' asked Salvatore again. 'Are you absolutely sure?'

'Absolutely.'

'Good grief!'

'On another occasion, Crates...'

The Professor broke off because at that moment his son-in-law entered the room looking like a beaten man. Tossing the brief-case containing all his publicity material for nuclear fall-out shelters into a corner, Giorgio dropped wearily into an armchair.

'Nothing doing?' asked Saverio.

'Nothing.'

'What did they say?'

'They said: "Who wants to live for ever? If there's a nuclear war, we stay right where we are. Everyone has to die sooner or later."'

'Did you tell them about Nato and the triple warheads?' Saverio wanted to know.

'Yes, but it made no impression.'

'Professò,' said Luigino, rising from his chair, 'would you permit a poetic utterance for the occasion? ... I've composed a little poem:

*Man was an ape, according to tradition,*
*then he invented wheels and went therefrom*
*to trains and aeroplanes and television,*
*and finally to the triple-headed bomb.*
*Which makes me wonder if man has progressed*
*or is, in point of fact, an utter pest!*

'How does he do it!' exclaimed Salvatore reverentially while the Colonel rose to congratulate Luigino.

'I've no idea,' replied Giorgio absent-mindedly. 'I only know that I'm wasting my time here in Naples. My chief worry is that Dr Frankfutter, general manager of Sicurat, is arriving from Switzerland in a day or two. What can I tell him? To have a good time?'

'You certainly haven't got the easiest thing to sell!' the Colonel remarked.

'I think,' said the Professor, 'that Neapolitans are temperamentally incapable of grasping the idea of dying collectively.'

'What do you mean?' asked Salvatore.

'A true Neapolitan, man of love that he is, has latched on to a fundamental fact, that death does not exist aside from the pain it gives to those left behind. Epicurus said as much himself: "Why should the thought of death frighten us? If you're alive you're not dead, and if you're dead you don't exist."'

'With all due respect to Epicurus,' remarked Salvatore, 'that saying strikes me as utter claptrap. How can death not exist?'

'What I mean,' explained Bellavista, 'is that the thought of a collective, total catastrophe would never worry a Neapolitan. Death without a tear being shed or a funeral arranged would strike him as being rather jolly. On the other hand, can you imagine the fate of a survivor? After one week in his shelter, what does the poor devil do? If he crawls out to have a look around, what will he see? Streets full of dead people, corpses on every side. Without aeroplanes or trains there's no way he can escape. He has no option but to return to his shelter. And where will he find food to survive?'

'My shelters,' put in Giorgio, 'are equipped with rations to last for six months.'

'And is it worth living an extra six months in an underground tomb?' asked Bellavista.

'Papà,' protested Giorgio, 'if everyone thought as you do, we wouldn't have sold millions of our shelters around the world. Do you know that there's a hospital in Lugano on three floors that's got another hospital on three floors underneath it to serve as a nuclear fall-out shelter? The one underneath is an exact copy of the one on top. There's a shelter for admissions on the ground floor, one for non-critical cases on the second and one for intensive care on the third.'

'Get that, Savè?' remarked Salvatore. 'In Switzerland they don't want to die even when they're at death's door! As I see it, if you're about to kick the bucket and there's nothing you can do about it, then make the most of the chance of dying in company with everyone else! But they apparently don't see it like that: they want to last as long as they possibly can, even if it means living in a sewer!'

'To be perfectly frank,' said the Colonel, 'I'm against nuclear fall-out shelters, too. Think what would happen in my case. I would only need the smallest shelter, a couple of rooms plus toilet for myself, my wife and the maid. But come the fateful day I'm as certain as certain can be that when I went down to the cellar I should find the entire Carratelli family of father, mother, mother-in-law and seven children huddling around the door of the shelter. The Carratellis live in the flat next to mine, on the same floor, and have done so for the last twelve years. The accountant is a nice, quiet person who has never in his life, as far as I can remember, ever asked me for anything, not a lemon or a corkscrew. But can you imagine what would happen on that day? He'd be sitting on the steps of the shelter and looking at me without saying a word but with a look in his eye saying more clearly than any words could do: You're saving your own skin and we are left here to die. And what can I do? I can't say, "Excuse me, please!" and slam the door behind me. No, my friend, you heed my words: as far as Naples is concerned, unless everyone has a shelter it just won't work.'

'So, Colonnè,' exclaimed Saverio, 'now you're making difficulties too! Our friend's already down in the dumps. Between you, you're going to make him give up altogether! But I've got a different idea. This is a matter of strategy, of marketing. Leave it up to Salvatore and me and we'll show you how to sell nuclear fall-out shelters.'

'When it comes to selling anything, I'm your man,' agreed Salvatore.

'So this is what we'll do,' said Saverio. 'Salvatore and I will prepare the ground by spreading panic...'

'Panic?' queried Giorgio.

'Yes,' continued Saverio, warming to his subject. 'We'll get everyone paranoid about nuclear warfare. We'll go around saying that we've been told by a certain Russian relative that Nato is about to be attacked. Then along comes the architect with a special introductory offer of ten economy-priced shelters.'

'When are they going to despatch the shelter from Switzerland?' asked Salvatore.

'Any day now,' replied Giorgio. 'They said by the end of the month at the latest.'

'Fine,' said Saverio. 'As soon as it arrives we'll transform the courtyard into a Nuclear Exhibition Centre. We'll have a big, big banner over the entrance, a poster showing the mushroom cloud, a hundred or so fairy lights in all the colours of the rainbow...'

'And hey presto it's Carnival!' moaned Giorgio despondently.

'Look,' said Salvatore encouragingly, 'you've got to sell nuclear fall-out shelters, right? So take it easy, you're in good hands. In one week Saverio and I will shift a dozen of 'em.'


Donn'Attilio Morace was a Neapolitan self-made man. Starting as a porter at the Garibaldi station, he had ended up selling records in Piazza Mercato. Without exaggeration, Donn'Attilio Morace could now, if he wanted to, paper his walls with banknotes to a value of five billion lire and not notice the difference. Despite this wealth, however, he still lived the life of an employee, dividing his time between home and shop, television and football. He liked to go to the cinema at Christmas and to take home a tray of pastries every Sunday. He was married but childless, and to make up for this had a mistress of thirteen years' standing for whom he now felt nothing more violent than affection; a second wife, one might say. He had no foibles apart from twenty cigarettes a day and a weekly flutter on the same three numbers in the Lotto which had never paid off but which he had played as a matter of principle for thirty years. 'Donn'Attì,' people would say, 'what are you going to do with all this money?' 'I don't know,' he would reply. And mean it.

Donn'Attilio was the first customer that Giorgio, Saverio and Salvatore targeted with their new strategy. He had the money, he had the land behind his house, too, so there was no excuse for his not buying a nuclear fall-out shelter.

'Donn'Attì,' began Saverio with an air of grave anxiety, 'I've got some bad news for you, I'm afraid. People are making preparations for the third world war.'

'How do you mean?'

'All the most industrialized nations are building nuclear fall-out shelters,' continued Saverio, 'and this could be very dangerous.'

'Why is that?'

'The reason we've avoided world wars for so long is because everyone's been too frightened. But now that the Western world has protected itself with nuclear fall-out shelters, what is there to stop it?'

'So what's your solution?'

'We've got to think about nuclear fall-out shelters for ourselves.'

'Actually,' said Donn'Attilio, 'we're all right because where I live we've got a cellar. During the last war the people living opposite used to come over too because it's one of those old cellars with walls five feet thick.'

'Donn'Attì,' Giorgio interposed, 'I don't mean to frighten you, but you can't compare the bombing in the last world war with a nuclear attack! When a nuclear bomb explodes, the temperature of the surrounding two kilometres goes up to three thousand degrees centigrade . . .'

'Four thousand degrees?' exclaimed Salvatore, horrified.

'No, three thousand,' repeated Giorgio.

'Ah, thank heaven for that!' said Salvatore, much relieved.

'As I was saying,' continued the architect, 'the temperature rises to three thousand degrees and the fireball burns everything in its path, trees, houses, people and so on. Then a shock wave develops...'

'Shock wave?' asked Donn'Attilio.

'Yes, a shock wave, a rush of air that lifts up houses as if they were pieces of paper. You could be sitting in your cellar one minute and the next there would be no building above your head!'

'Holy Mother of God protect us!' gasped Saverio.

'So how much would a small shelter for two people cost?'

'Here we are: model Nuclear 02,' said Giorgio, pulling a folder from his brief-case, 'measuring forty-two square metres and comprising entrance with shower, living room, two bunk beds, corner kitchen, bathroom and emergency exit. The price of thirty-five million lire plus VAT includes ventilation system, overalls, masks, rations for six months and the cost of installation.'

A prolonged silence underlined the tension as they waited for Donn'Attilio's first reaction. Giorgio searched his face anxiously while Salvatore could not help remembering that only last week Donn'Attilio had told him of his decision not to change his ancient 131 for a new car simply because the new one had electric windows and he only felt at home with a handle.

'Tell me one thing,' said Donn'Attilio. 'This business of ventilation. I don't know anything about nuclear war but surely, when a bomb explodes, all the air around is contaminated, so where does the fresh air come from?'

'Of course you're right, the air is contaminated,' Giorgio replied expertly, 'but the Zot system contains a filter that excludes all alpha, beta and gamma rays.'

'Even the gamma rays?'

'Indeed, Donn'Attì,' interrupted Salvatore smoothly, 'and I've seen the system in action. It's not electrical, it's a gadget that you have to work by turning a handle.'

'How much does it come to per square metre?'

'A fraction over a million,' replied Giorgio, his hopes of a deal rising.

'A mere trifle!' exclaimed Salvatore helpfully.

Another pause, another agonizing wait. Then, at last, Donn'Attilio spoke.

'I'm in a difficult situation, you see. I would actually need two shelters quite close to each other, one for me and my wife and one for a lady who lives near here, in the next building.'

'For Donna Margherita?' asked Salvatore, without a shadow of reticence.

'Yes, for Donna Margherita. Now, you would have to arrange for a tube ... or whatever ... a kind of underground passageway from one to the other, so that I could spend part of my time in this one and part in that.'

'Donn'Attì,' said Giorgio helpfully, 'why don't you have a larger shelter and all three use it? You could order Nuclear 05, with four bunk beds.'

'Because in that case the air outside would be much healthier than the air inside.'

'I see. But even if you had two separate shelters, it wouldn't be necessary to link them with a passage because you can always leave the shelter whenever you like, provided, of course, that you wear the protective suit. The important thing to remember is that you must wash in the shower provided for that purpose every time you enter the shelter.'

'So everything'll be fine, Donn'Attì,' said Saverio, summing up, 'as long as you remember that every time you visit Donna Margherita you have to wash before and after your visit. A bit of a bore, maybe, but at least it means you can do without an underground passage.'

'This coming Saturday, at No. 58 Via Petrarca, we shall have the pleasure of demonstrating a Sicurat Nuclear 02 shelter to you,' announced Giorgio with pride. 'It will be the first nuclear fall-out shelter to be installed in Naples. The demonstration will start at 1600 hours precisely.'

'I shall certainly be there, and I'll bring my wife along too,' said Donn'Attilio. 'But please don't mention my having asked about two shelters.'

'Don't worry about that,' said Giorgio, immensely pleased with the way things had gone.

'Incidentally, there's something else I should like to know. Am I right in thinking that these shelters could also be used in peacetime while we're waiting for war to break out?'

'Of course they can,' Giorgio assented. 'Were you thinking about using one as a storeroom?'

'Storeroom, hidey-hole, maybe even underground factory, if you see what I mean.'

'No reason why you shouldn't,' replied Giorgio, not yet understanding what Donn'Attilio had in mind.

'You see, at the moment I use that cellar I was telling you about for producing pirate cassettes and blue films, but it isn't all that safe. At night the light can be seen from outside and when the music's too loud it can be heard. I'm always afraid of the police catching me, to say nothing about my wife's jealous rages when she accuses me of watching dirty films. So it occurred to me that if these shelters are even proof against gamma rays, they ought to be proof against my wife and the police.'

The nuclear fall-out shelter arrived suddenly one morning. Eight o'clock had not yet struck when an enormous trailer preceded by two police motor-cyclists pulled up outside the entrance in Via Petrarca. The unusual load immediately attracted the attention of the passers-by and despite the early hour the courtyard was soon thronged with a large crowd of curious people. Anyone who knows Naples can imagine the comments of the Neapolitans: everyone wanted to see, touch, ask questions about and get into the shelter.

The long and laborious unloading operation took up practically the entire morning. Finally, however, there it was installed in the middle of the courtyard. Along either side was written, in large letters: NUCLEAR FALL-OUT SHELTER SICURAT MOD. NUCLEAR 02 LUGANO.

The shape of the shelter was that of a vast pink parallelepiped thirteen metres long and three wide, with a cylindrical cabin at the front entered via an escape hatch like that of a submarine. A silver ventilation pipe ran along the right-hand side, and on the roof, towards the rear, was another circular hatch bearing the legend: EMERGENCY EXIT. From a distance, the general appearance was similar to Piccard's 'bathyscaphe'.

Salvatore, dubbing himself 'nuclear manager', had his hands full keeping the local residents at a safe distance. At one point he was obliged to shut the main door from the street and allow access only to those with a genuine right of passage, meaning residents and the well heeled. Even so, as the days passed by the shelter began to look less and less like a miracle of Swiss engineering and more and more like a Neapolitan container-home. The children adopted it as a space ship and played on it from morning to night, Rachelina tied one end of her washing line to it, and there were even those who had the forethought, with the coming nuclear war in mind, to attach a couple of adhesive stickers of the Bleeding Heart of Jesus right beside the name of Sicurat.

The demonstration was arranged for 13 June, St Anthony's Day. Giorgio had commissioned a sign-writer to paint a great banner with the words THERE IS STILL TIME, and a printer from Port'Alba to produce a poster showing a family enjoying a meal in their shelter just as a nuclear bomb exploded over the Gulf of Naples. Every possible prospective customer (starting with Donn'Attilio) had been invited as well as friends, journalists and a local TV station. And finally, eagerly awaited by the entire district, the great day itself arrived.

The anti-nuclear day began punctually at 1600 hours with a showing of Alain Resnais' film *Hiroshima, mon amour* in the parish hall of the nearby church of San Domenico. Giorgio had tried to book *The Day After* but had failed. However, *Hiroshima, mon amour* was just as good an introduction to the subject. The only problem had been to convince the priest that it was not a blue movie.

The demonstration itself began around half past six. Every inhabitant from the surrounding area would have liked to get into the courtyard, but a strict pecking-order, organized by Salvatore, permitted entry only to those who could afford to order a shelter. Those who were curious but poor found themselves shut out of the courtyard behind a paling from where they could only see, and that with difficulty, the top of the shelter and the entrance hatches bearing the name Sicurat.

One old lady, having had a good look at the posters showing the mushroom cloud over Vesuvius, approached Don Ferdinando.

'Don Ferdinà, all this talk about a nuclear bomb isn't because someone's discovered that another world war's about to break out, is it? Are we in danger, do you think? Have you heard anything?'

'Signò,' replied Don Ferdinando with an air of total indifference, 'I know nothing about it, but even if war breaks out I shan't give it a second thought. No one's ever going to get me into a nuclear shelter. If I'm going to die, I intend to die sitting down!'

On a bench in one corner of the courtyard Salvatore and Rachelina had laid out all the accessories and articles of clothing that would be needed in the case of a nuclear war. There were yellow overalls, gas masks, anti-contamination powders, torches, first-aid kits and everything else that could possibly aid survival in a time of crisis. There was even a kind of exercise bicycle which could be used, by vigorous pedalling, to power a generator.

'Signò,' explained Rachelina to one of the tenants, 'when a nuclear bomb explodes, the main danger isn't so much the iron bomb that could fall on your head, but the *fall-off* you get with every explosion. I was told by a lady who lives in Materdei, who has a cousin who lives in Japan and understands these things, that the smell is quite awful, that's why one simply has to put on a gas mask. Then you see this powder? That's used for nuclear decontamination. If atoms start crawling up your skirts, you can kill them all with this powder, one by one.'

Three unemployed friends of Salvatore's walked round and round the shelter wearing overalls and gas masks until one of them, the oldest, felt unwell and removed his gas mask, asking Giorgio to excuse him any further involvement.

'Forgive me, sir,' said the poor man, 'but I'm about to suffocate inside that contraption. I can't breathe!'

In the porter's lodge, Saverio had assumed the *ad hoc* role of professor of nuclear physics. Grasping a sheet of paper, he was explaining the working of a nuclear bomb to a group of tenants all greatly alarmed by the word 'megaton'.

'What I am about to show you,' said Saverio professorially, drawing a long wavy line on a piece of cardboard, 'is nothing less than the famous chain reaction invented by the Italian scientist Enrico Fermi. Very simply, here is the chain that leads to the explosion of a ten megaton nuclear bomb. The atoms travel along this line until they reach a bend here, at this point. Then, because it's a bend, the atoms collide with each other and the collision causes the first explosion: BANG. The same thing happens every time they meet a bend on their way: BANG, BANG, BANG, until you get the final explosion: BOOMMM.'

'But that's not an atomic bomb, that's a squib!' exclaimed Capuozzo.

'But much louder,' assented Saverio.

Standing in front of the shelter and possibly inspired by the pink paint, Luigino was crooning softly: *'na casarella / pittata rosa / 'ncoppe 'e Camaldole / vurria tenè ... / peccerenella / p' 'o sposo e 'a sposa / comme a 'na connola / pe mme e pe tte ...*'[2]

Luigino's performance was interrupted by the arrival of the priest to bless the shelter. Everyone made the sign of the cross. One or two turned their gaze fervently heavenwards. These were presumably people who, finding themselves in temporary difficulties and with no immediate prospects of providing themselves with fall-out shelters, were seeking an alternative means of protection.

Giorgio, meanwhile, stayed unwaveringly beside Donn'Attilio. Gripping his arm, he expatiated on the virtues of the shelter.

'Donn'Attì, as a man involved in commerce I'm sure you know more than me about how the Swiss do things. They only use materials of the best possible quality. Let me introduce you

---

2 'A little house / all painted pink / above Camaldoli / that's what I'd like ... / a tiny house / for a man and his bride / a cot / for you and me ...'

to my general manager, Dr Frankfutter, who can also assure you about that.'

Smiling, Frankfutter shook Donn'Attilio's hand and, speaking with a pronounced German accent, confirmed Giorgio's statement.

'All the materials used have been tested in our Lugano laboratory as is required by Swiss law, and every one carries a guarantee which will never expire.'

'Excuse me for interrupting,' objected the ubiquitous Capuozzo, 'but this matter of the guarantee seems to me like so much eyewash! You're not telling me that a man can pick up the phone "the day after" as the American film title has it and say: "Excuse me, but everything's cracking up and we've got bits of the nuclear bomb in here!"'

Frankfutter, puzzled perhaps by the Neapolitan dialect, said nothing, and Giorgio, having shot a dark look at Capuozzo, decided to introduce Frankfutter to Bellavista.

'Doctor, may I present my father-in-law, Professor Bellavista.'

'*Molto piacere. Frankfutter*,' said the Swiss with a slight inclination of his head. 'Giorgio is a very able man and has a great future ahead of him.'

'A great future?' echoed Bellavista, his tone indicating a measure of incredulity.

'Indeed. Giorgio has a great future,' repeated Frankfutter. He pronounced Giorgio's name as *Chorcho*. 'My dear Professor, the entire Western hemisphere is now planning to protect itself with fall-out shelters. Calculations have shown that should a world war break out, the simultaneous explosion of 1,245 nuclear bombs would cause the destruction of all forms of life on the planet for at least five years. The human race could only survive by means of an adequate network of underground shelters. Against that day we expect to sell at least two million shelters in Italy, and our Chorcho will be able to earn a great deal of money in this field.'

'All of which he will spend underground,' concluded Bellavista.

The response made Giorgio resolve to avoid any further exchange of ideas between his general manager and the local population. Apart from anything else, Frankfutter's forecast of calamity, far from helping to persuade Donn'Attilio to buy a shelter, had had a depressing effect on the entrepreneur.

'Architè,' said Donn'Attilio, 'shall I tell you what I really think? If this is all we can look forward to, I'd rather drop dead now and there's an end to the matter.'

'Don't say such a thing even in jest!' retorted Giorgio. 'We have a duty to survive! Don't worry, when you see the shelter you'll see how beautifully it's been equipped.'

At a sign from the architect, Salvatore leaned a little wooden ladder, specially made for the purpose, against the shelter and climbed on to the top of the parallelepiped. Meanwhile, Giorgio picked up a microphone and addressed the crowd of onlookers:

'Ladies and gentlemen, may I have your attention for a moment. Three at a time, you may now enter the shelter. Please do not crowd the entrance: stand well back. Everyone will be able to see inside sooner or later.' Then, turning to Salvatore: 'Salvatò, open up.'

A sudden hush fell on the crowd as the deputy-assistant porter tried to raise the cover of the escape hatch. After a dozen attempts, Salvatore shouted:

'Architè! The door's jammed, it won't open!'

'Don't talk nonsense,' replied Giorgio. 'Turn the handle right round!'

'I did, but it won't open. It seems to be fastened on the inside.'

'Wait, I'll come up.'

Giorgio climbed on to the roof, but no matter how hard he wrestled with it, the cover refused to budge.

'Hey! Just a moment, Architè!' said Salvatore, 'Everyone keep quiet! I think I heard sounds coming from inside the shelter.'

Salvatore put his lips to the ventilation pipe and shouted: 'Is anyone in there?'

'Engaged,' replied a metallic voice from inside.

'Who by?'

'Me.'

Giorgio, with a sudden burst of anger, pushed Salvatore impatiently aside and yelled down the pipe with all the force of his lungs: 'Come out of there at once or I'll call the police!'

'No,' replied the hidden voice. 'I shall only come out if you all get off the top of the shelter and remove the ladder.'

Giorgio was momentarily nonplussed, then, realizing that he had little choice in the matter, climbed down with Salvatore. When the ladder had been removed, Salvatore knocked three times on the side wall.

'Hey there! . . . We're all down! Now come out!'

A few seconds elapsed and nothing happened. Giorgio called two policemen to his side. The cameraman from the local TV company got as close as he could to record the exit of the mysterious occupant of the fall-out shelter. At last the hatch cover was raised and a tall, thin man emerged.

'That's Mercalli!' yelled Salvatore, recognizing his cousin.

'Yes sir!' replied the man on the top of the shelter. 'Antonio Scalese, Salvatore's cousin, generally called Mercalli. Yesterday evening I was evicted from the container which was repossessed by Later & Co. because they had not been paid by the Council. My wife is here too and my children, Peppino, Francuccio and Sisina. Come here, children!'

One at a time, to the amazement of the crowd, three tall, thin children of whose paternity there could be no doubt whatsoever, emerged through the hatchway. Each was clutching a half-empty tin of jam.

'Supplies for six months!' groaned Giorgio, covering his eyes in despair.

'I hardly need tell you,' Antonio Scalese continued in a loud voice, 'that I have no intention of leaving this home. If you really want to know what I think of the shelter, I have to admit that it is, unfortunately, not very comfortable. There are no windows and it's extremely hot and airless. On the other hand, I've got no choice, and until the Council offers me adequate accommodation I shall have to make do.'

One of the policemen picked up the ladder and took a step or two towards the shelter.

'Stay right there!' shouted Scalese, pushing his family hastily back through the hatchway. 'I advise the agents of law and order not to attempt to evict me by force. The shelter is, as they say, "bomb-proof", and according to the Swiss brochure we have six months' supply of food.' Then he turned to Giorgio reprovingly: 'Only one thing's missing: coffee.'

Giorgio spread his arms in a gesture of apology.

'Now, correct me if I'm mistaken,' continued Mercalli, 'but if a Swiss family can live for six months on these supplies, a Neapolitan family can live on them for a year at least.'

'My dear sir,' Frankfutter interrupted, 'I must inform you that our shelter may only be inhabited in time of war.'

'And I, my dear sir,' replied Mercalli, imitating the German accent, 'must inform you that as far as I am concerned, war has already been declared!'

# Socrates and the UFOs

SOCRATES Greetings, Eupolymus, it's good to see you again after all this time. If my memory is correct, at least three months have passed since you departed for Larissa.

EUPOLYMUS Exactly three months, O Socrates. The last time we met was on the fourth day of the festival of Panathenaea. I still remember how we went straight from the Acropolis to Philoxenus' house where, after a glass of excellent Tachos, you spoke to me about the Gods and about fate who, you said, was the most important of all the Gods.

SOCRATES Why did you stay in your native city so long this time? Was it not you who accused the Thessalians of being lazy and superficial?

EUPOLYMUS Indeed, but I was delayed for a very sad reason. My father died, and as my brothers are not yet of age I had to attend to all the family business.

SOCRATES I am indeed distressed to hear that. Please accept my condolences, although belated.

EUPOLYMUS In the final analysis it was no real tragedy, O Socrates, since my father was an old man and life had given him all he asked of it.

CRITO Forgive me for interrupting, O Eupolymus, but I too am an old man and have always enjoyed my life, yet my sons would be sad to see me die.

EUPOLYMUS Not only your sons, O Crito, but all the just men of Athens would mourn your passing.

SOCRATES Tell me, Eupolymus, how did you find the Thessalians this time?

EUPOLYMUS Just the same as ever, O Socrates. First they invent something, then they pronounce it to be true. One of my fellow-citizens, for example, a certain Prestiphoremus, swears that one night, when he was walking among the olive trees, he met an extraterrestrial being in flesh and blood...

CRITO An extraterrestrial being?

EUPOLYMUS Yes, a little green man with two eyes in front and two behind, and a swivelling ear on top of his head for picking up signals. So the Thessalians, instead of treating the whole thing as a joke, as they should have done, believed the man and showered him with gifts. The rogue now refuses to work his land, preferring to live at the state's expense and tell his story over and over again. I heard that for two minae he will even draw you a picture of his alien on a tablet.

SOCRATES How extraordinary it is that beings from other planets are always described as green and never any other colour!

EUPOLYMUS Probably to distinguish them better from us earthlings. If someone said he'd seen a yellow alien, people might object that all he'd seen was a Chinese!

CRITO Anaxagoras, who's an expert in celestial matters, says that so far there have been more than two hundred thousand reported sightings of UFOs, and that in the forest of Oreos on the island of Euboea people have seen gigantic footprints the shape of a chicken's foot.

SOCRATES If a man reports having seen flying saucers and little green men on his walks through the woods, and if this man is one worthy of our respect, I see no reason why we should not believe his word. All the same, it does seem strange that these mysterious beings should have visited this planet more than two hundred thousand times only to vanish without trace. You, O Eupolymus, left Larissa this morning and I assume it took you quite a while to drive to Athens.

EUPOLYMUS Five hours and ten minutes on the motorway.

SOCRATES But you did not, as soon as you came within sight of the walls of Themistocles, change your mind and drive back the way you had come?

EUPOLYMUS I wouldn't dream of it, O Socrates. I came to Athens with a specific purpose in mind, which was to see you and Crito.

SOCRATES Aliens too, one must assume, would have had some specific purpose, otherwise they would never have set out upon such a long journey in the first place. I would imagine them as being involved with research into galactic civilizations, or at least as being interested in the thousand and one questions natural to space explorers: resources as yet undiscovered, strange inventions, different foodstuffs, local customs and traditions and so on and so forth. And yet, according to the testimony of those who assert the presence of extraterrestrial beings on earth, all these aliens, after an extremely tedious journey lasting two or three thousand years, have apparently revealed themselves for a few seconds to some nondescript peasant and then immediately started on a return voyage.

EUPOLYMUS It does seem unlikely.

SOCRATES It's as if Christopher Columbus, approaching the shores of America, had waited only for the boy's shout of 'Land ahoy!' before turning to his crew and saying, 'Well done, lads, now let's get straight back to Spain otherwise Queen Isabella will be worried about us,' while, at that very moment, some native was running to his chief to report that he'd just seen three caravels from outer space.

CRITO Are you saying, O Socrates, that we are the only inhabitants of the Universe?

SOCRATES I should never venture to say that, O Crito. Indeed, if you really want to know what I think, I believe that there are thousands, perhaps millions, of inhabited planets in the Universe, but because the distance between them is so immense, they cannot communicate with each other. Democritus told me one day that there can be no life on the planets which lie nearest to us. Mercury is but a ball of fire, and the same applies to Venus where the temperatures rise to over a thousand degrees. And as for the planets beyond Mars, they are colder than the glaciers in the Caucasus because they are so far from the sun. So, to find conditions comparable to our own, we would have perforce to extend our search beyond our own solar system and into another.

CRITO What would the centre of this other solar system be?

SOCRATES A star called Alpha Centauri. According to Democritus, it's so close to us that if you observe it from a different point in the Galaxy, it would appear to be joined to our Sun in the same way that those who have very good eyesight assert to be the case with Mizar and its twin star.

EUPOLYMUS If that is so, is it not possible that, at a given distance from this star, there could be a planet similar to our own, having the same temperature and the same atmosphere and another Socrates who, at this very moment, is discussing the possibility of our existence?

SOCRATES It is most likely, but it would take us so long, so very long (one hundred thousand years one way and one hundred thousand years the other) to reach this planet that no traveller would ever be able to tell us about the marvels he had seen. That is why I am convinced that when men first make contact with beings from other planets, it will not be a close encounter but by radio astronomy. Some day, one of the many radio telescopes directed at outer space will receive a signal distinct from all the others. When that happens, our astronomers will set about deciphering it and then transmit their own message using the same code.

EUPOLYMUS How would you explain the fact, O Socrates, that so many people swear they have seen aliens and spoken to them?

SOCRATES The human soul needs to sustain itself with hope in the same way that the stomach has need of food. But life is often sad and human desires go unrequited. Some conditions have no cure: we must all die, an ugly person cannot become beautiful, an old one cannot regain youth, and those whose lives are dull and unenlivened by enthusiasm know that they will probably never change for the better. So what can be done? Nothing except take comfort in things mystical, in the supernatural. Thus it is that stories, myths, sightings of extraterrestrial beings, horoscopes, drug-taking and extremist political parties flourish. As soon as a market is identified, someone will supply it. People ready to take advantage of the misery of others, like soothsayers, demagogues, drug-pushers and sellers of lottery tickets, spring up like mushrooms.

EUPOLYMUS But what can we do about such people?

SOCRATES They must be chased from the temples! I'm too old now for such battles. It is up to men like you, Eupolymus, you who are young and strong.

EUPOLYMUS I am always grateful to you for your advice and your words of wisdom. But now I must leave you, O Socrates, and Crito too, regretfully, because I have an appointment to meet Simmias the Theban outside the Apollo Cinema ... Tonight is the world première of *The Return to Earth of ET*, and Simmias and I do not want to arrive late.

# The Double

'So who was the first person to organize the Olympic Games, Professor?' asked Salvatore.

'No one really knows,' replied Bellavista. 'The origins are, as they say, lost in the mists of antiquity. Some give the credit to Hercules, others to Achilles, and some say they were started by Iphitus, King of Elis, in 776 BC.'

The Professor and his disciples had just returned from their usual afternoon walk, taking them from Via Petrarca, along Via Manzoni, through the Memorial Gardens and back again after a rest and a coffee at the Miramare. Although only the middle of January, the sky was a vivid blue and crystal clear, the temperature so mild that spring seemed to have arrived already. Our group of peripatetics, led, of course, by the Professor talking volubly, entered through the archway and settled in the porter's lodge to continue the discussion.

'Greece at the time was a universe in miniature,' declared Bellavista as soon as he was ensconced in his usual armchair. 'You might imagine it as so many scattered, smallish towns, each about the size of Afragola, and all constantly at war among themselves. It was a practical impossibility to avoid a quarrel with some neighbour in the course of a lifetime. The slaves worked from morning to night and the citizens did the only thing they were capable of doing: they went to war! Imagine, young Spartans, not knowing what to do with themselves in the evening during the rare intervals of peace, used to free a dozen or so slaves and then hunt them throughout the night. The first to catch them, killed them.'

'But what about those who weren't fit enough for that kind of life?' asked Saverio.

'They were regarded as a lower form of life,' replied Bellavista, 'and as like as not done away with at birth.'

'Goodness gracious me!' exclaimed Salvatore, deeply shocked.

'Salvatò,' teased Saverio, as quick as a flash, 'they'd have dumped you in a plastic sack without a second thought.'

'One of the many little city states was Elis,' continued Bellavista, 'which lay right next door to Sparta, the most warlike of all the cities. One day the Elian king, Iphitus, very uneasy about his belligerent neighbours, said to his people: "Look, lads, we're in the devil of a cleft stick: either we've got to prepare for war with the Spartans, in which case we're in for a hiding, or we've got to acknowledge their military superiority, in which case they'll make us live like themselves. The only way out of this is to declare our region sacred to the Gods." So they gradually put it about that Jove had played in the forests of Elis as a child and that Hercules had won a wrestling match against his brothers there. It was enough, and once the formula for survival had been established, they had no more problems. The city of Olympus was declared neutral territory, and every four years all the Greek states sent their most able champions to compete against each other. While the games were in progress, all wars were suspended.'

'It was only the men who competed, wasn't it?' asked Saverio.

'Women were even barred from watching, on pain of death! A woman called Callipatira who very much wanted to see her son compete did once manage to get in, disguised as a trainer. But when the boy won, her tearful hugs and kisses alerted everyone to the fact that she was a woman. From that day on, it became a rule that everyone attending the games should do so stark naked.'

'Were the athletes well rewarded?'

'Indeed they were! An Olympic win was enough to set a man up for life, and not only him but his descendants as well. They earned so much that many philosophers, including Xenophon and Plato, complained bitterly about brawn ranking higher than brain in Greece.'

'Just like now, in fact, Professor,' remarked Salvatore. 'Footballers have lived better than university professors since time began. Take the case of Maradona. People here in Naples sometimes don't know where their next meal is coming from, yet we go out and buy the most expensive footballer in the world!'

'To be honest, Professor,' chipped in Saverio, 'this business about the people in Naples being poor doesn't altogether convince me. I have the impression that there are very few of us left who are really poor, while all the rest are rolling in money.'

'What on earth has suddenly given you that idea?' asked Salvatore, surprised.

'Well, you see, Salvatò, I've always reckoned that Neapolitans are wealthier than they make themselves out to be. Look at all the cars, the colour televisions, the number of people who go to a restaurant in the evening. But my positive proof comes from the rubbish.'

'The rubbish?'

'Absolutely. The rubbish,' repeated Saverio. 'Look, I'm not one to boast, but when it comes to rubbish I'm an expert. I've been a refuse collector for five years now, and believe me, I could tell you all about the life-style of a family from the rubbish they put out, without even opening the plastic sack. If I were the Finance Minister the first thing I'd do to assess tax liability is check the rubbish of every taxpayer. Under the present system the inspectors estimate the average liability of a city from the declarations people make, so naturally Naples is at the bottom of the list.'

'Professor,' said Luigi, standing up, 'may I offer a poetic contribution?

*From Alpine peak to pyramid,*
*from the Pyrenees to Bihar,*
*if I rummage in your rubbish-bin*
*I'll know you for what you are!*

Just at that moment, there was a tremendous hubbub in the street outside: clapping, shouts of 'hooray!', the hooting of car horns. Salvatore got up and went to see what was happening. He returned a few moments later with his eyes popping out of his head.

'Professor, Maradona's out there! Maradona in flesh and blood! He's being mobbed by autograph hunters. There must be more than a hundred of...'

Before Salvatore could finish the sentence a group of people headed by Maradona with his manager and a photographer, burst into the porter's lodge.

'*Calmense muchachos, calmense: nada de autógrafos!*' shouted the Argentinian escort, interposing himself bodily between Maradona and the crowd. Then, turning to Bellavista and the others he said apologetically: '*Señores, perdónenme por la invasión.*'

'*Priego,*' replied Salvatore politely, trying to speak Spanish.

'*Por favor,*' continued the Argentinian, addressing Salvatore, '*le diga a los tifosos que Dieguito no puede conceder autógrafos. Pueden solo sacarte algunas fotos si entran uno a la vez.*'[1]

Maradona appeared to be thoroughly frightened. But his manager kept his nerve, allowing admittance only to those who wanted their photos taken with the champion. A queue formed outside the door. Salvatore was paid ten thousand lire to keep order. The photographer insisted on being paid in advance as people entered: five thousand per photograph with the assurance that when they were printed, each copy would be signed by Maradona.

'*Quante sì bello Dieghito!*' shouted a fan, trying to embrace his hero. '*Tu ce 'a fà vencere 'o campionato!*'[2]

'*Rapido, señor,*' Maradona begged him, struggling to free himself, '*rapido que tengo que volver a casa.*'[3]

To speed matters up, the fans were brought in two at a time. Each couple hardly had time for a quick handshake before the flashbulb popped and they were hustled out. Eventually another Argentinian appeared shouting:

---

[1] 'Please tell the fans that Diego will not sign any autographs. But he will allow photographs to be taken if they come in one at a time.'
[2] 'You're wonderful, Diego!... You'll win us the cup!'
[3] 'Quickly, please, ... I'm anxious to get home.'

'*Vamos, Maradona, vamos!*'[4]

In the twinkling of an eye, as they had come in so everyone vanished, and a few moments later Inspector Di Domenico and his sergeant Colapietro walked into the porter's lodge.

'Good afternoon, Professor,' said the Inspector. 'How long has that fake Maradona been gone?'

'Less than five minutes,' replied Bellavista matter-of-factly. 'I saw through him straight away but I was curious to see what would happen.'

'Commissà,' said Rachelina, Salvatore's wife, brandishing a percolator, 'would you like a coffee?'

'We really ought to be on our way,' replied the Inspector, tempted to stay and chat with the Professor.

'Commissà,' prompted his sergeant, 'why bother? The Sorrentino brothers have got away and there's nothing we can do about it for the moment. It would be more interesting to identify that photographer. Salvatore could give us a description.'

'Who are these people?' asked Bellavista.'

'Small fry. It's only a case of petty fraud,' remarked Di Domenico with mild distaste. 'They're brothers by the name of Sorrentino and they've all been inside on various occasions for minor misdemeanours such as fiddling, card-sharping and general jiggery-pokery. One month ago, over Christmas, they finally landed an honest job of work when the youngest of the brothers, Vincenzino, decided to cash in on a certain resemblance to Maradona and charged people for being photographed with him in Villa Communale. You know how kids love being photographed with Father Christmas. Well, this year, because of the unemployment situation, there were more Father Christmases than children, so the idea of being photographed with Maradona instead worked very well indeed. But Christmas doesn't last for ever, and the brothers Sorrentino reckoned they were on to something too good to drop, so they went on with the photographs but they were now passing off Vincenzino for the

[4] 'Come on, Maradona, let's get going!'

real Maradona. If it were up to me I'd let them get on with it, but unfortunately I've received some official complaints and I've got to take some action.'

'Who's complained?' asked Bellavista.

'It's all rather complicated,' began the Inspector, who had now decided to stay put for the next half hour at least. 'My dear Professor, the position is this. When Maradona – who's a great lad – first came here, a very important business organization came with him called "Maradona Production" which has the sole right to pictures of the Argentinian footballer. The business transacted by this company has an American name that I can't pronounce correctly because I don't speak English, but it sounds like *marciandis* or *marciandais*[5] or something of the sort. Anyway, to put it simply it means that if you buy a mug or whatever with Maradona's face on it, "Maradona Production" is entitled to a percentage of the price.'

'Well, how about that!' exclaimed Salvatore. 'They don't miss a trick, do they!'

'But now what's happened?' Di Domenico continued. 'Everyone concerned with "Maradona Production" is up in arms because when they arrived in Naples after a month's delay they found everything that could possibly be done with Maradona's face had already been done by the Neapolitans. You couldn't go anywhere without seeing it. Maradona's face on the cover of children's exercise books, Maradona's head with red eyes that lit up with the brake lights in the back of cars, Maradona knickers, Maradona sweatshirts, Maradona towels and jars of tomatoes with lids sporting a picture of Maradona against a background of 'Napoli blue'. In Borgo Sant'Antonio Abate there's even a stall selling Maradona wigs, which means that every time you see a group of kids playing football in the street, it's like watching a match between twenty-two Maradonas.'

'Naples can shift itself surprisingly quickly when there's a chance of earning a bit of hard cash!' Salvatore exclaimed with pride.

---

[5] i.e. 'merchandise'.

'It's the age-old art of expediency that pops up whenever there is a chink of light,' remarked the Professor. 'That too is something we owe to the Greeks.'

'In what way, Professor?' asked the Inspector.

'In Greece, expediency even had its own deity. He was called Poros, or "Contrivance", or, if you prefer it, the art of the main chance,' explained the Professor. 'And the poorer people invoked him whenever they were in trouble. Plato tells us about him in one of the most fascinating of his dialogues, the *Symposium*.'

The name of Plato acting like a signal, everyone gathered around the Professor to hear better. Plato had an enthusiastic following in the porter's lodge of 58, Via Petrarca, where Bellavista's stories had made him a household name.

'The subject is Love,' Bellavista began, 'and in the dialogue Plato makes each one present give an opinion about it. When Socrates' turn comes, he tells us how Love was born.'

'The Professor's a great devotee of Socrates,' whispered Salvatore confidentially to the Inspector.

'Socrates describes how all the Gods of Olympus were invited to a great banquet to celebrate the birth of Aphrodite. All, that is, except the goddess Poverty, who had been excluded simply because she was poor.'

'Aha!' exclaimed Salvatore. 'The Olympian Gods are just like a family I know, the relatives of Baron Santorsola Davalós, every one a toffee-nosed snob!'

'Almost identical,' agreed Bellavista. 'However, Poverty went along all the same, but she stayed outside the door of...'

'... of the restaurant...' suggested Salvatore.

'... of the place where the banquet was being held, hoping that someone would throw her a morsel of food. Now Contrivance had drunk a good deal of nectar that evening, in fact he was almost drunk, so there came a point when he decided to go out for a breath of fresh air. But as soon as he was outside, the freshness of the air made him giddy and he fainted right at the feet of Poverty. The Goddess now realized that if she grabbed her chance she could solve all her problems at a stroke. She thought: "Here at my feet lies Poros, the God of Contrivance, the most cunning of all the Gods. Only such a God as this can help me!" So without wasting any time, she coupled with him and of their union Love was born.'

'They did that outside the banqueting hall?' exclaimed Salvatore in amazement.

'The tale has a moral,' the Professor continued. 'Socrates thought of Love as the child of Poverty, an idea of which Jesus would have approved, but also as the child of Contrivance, which is almost a Darwinian concept. Socrates says that Love is not a beautiful youth himself, but, because he was conceived on the day that Aphrodite was born, he is a lover of beauty. And he adds: "He is wretched, shoeless and homeless, always sleeping rough, on the ground, on doorsteps and in the street, because he takes after his mother and is always poor. But because he also takes after his father, he always schemes to get for himself whatever is noble; he is brave, daring, resolute, a great hunter, always ready to devise stratagems of all kinds, a lover of wisdom, full of resource, ever ready to philosophize, a dreadful swindler, a magician and true sophist." '

The long quotation almost evoked a round of applause from the assembled company. Di Domenico, in particular, was fascinated.

'So, Professor,' he remarked, 'it seems that Plato put together an identikit picture of the Neapolitan *mariunciello* many centuries before Naples itself was founded! But what I still don't understand is what all this has to do with Love.'

'As far as Socrates was concerned, Love could only come from Necessity. And now I'll show you why,' said Bellavista, rising to his feet. 'If Salvatore were to go outside and find a wallet containing ten billion lire, in cash, lying in the road, what would he do?'

'*Foss'a Madonna!*' exclaimed Salvatore, his eyes shining at the idea of finding a wallet stuffed with money. Then, thinking that maybe fulfilment of the prediction could be jeopardized by excessive greed, he added: 'Let's make it a million and a half, Professor; ten billion is a bit over the top.'

'No, it's got to be ten billion,' countered Bellavista, raising his voice. 'Now you tell me, my dear Salvatore, how your life would change if you picked up ten billion lire this very moment.'

'It's impossible!' replied Salvatore naïvely.

'Forget about whether it's impossible or not!' snapped the Professor, almost losing patience. 'Answer the question. What would you do if, at this very moment, you had ten billion lire in your pocket?'

Salvatore looked around, nonplussed. Finding his mind a blank, he looked at Saverio for help. Then, in a low voice, almost shyly, he said:

'I'd buy a flat.'

'A flat with ten billion? Only a flat? Surely you'd buy a fine villa at least!'

'Yes, yes, a villa, a villa!' echoed the others.

'It's only logical, Professor, that he must buy a villa,' insisted Saverio, treating the hypothesis as fact. 'Salvatore can't live in a condominium as if he were just anybody! Not with ten billion lire! He's going to buy a splendid, three-storeyed villa in Posillipo, with a private beach, a guest flat for his friends and a park around it where we can all go for wonderful walks together.

'A villa with a wrought-iron gate?' asked the Professor, pressing ever harder.

'A wrought-iron gate?' exclaimed Saverio, pre-empting an answer from Salvatore, the neo-billionaire, himself. 'Of course, and at least five metres high. Then we want a wall all around the property with barbed wire on top and an alarm system. We can't be too careful with ten billion lying around! If I were Salvatore I'd have a dozen Dobermanns patrolling the grounds, too.'

'And some guards as well,' said the Inspector. 'We mustn't overlook the risk of kidnap.'

'Something I'd really like,' said Salvatore diffidently, 'would be a secretary.'

'Excellent,' said Bellavista, ending the discussion. 'So, from what you have said I gather that as soon as Salvatore becomes a billionaire, anyone wishing to contact him will first have to ring the bell at the gate, then talk to the guards, then to his secretary, then with the Dobermanns and only then will be able to see him! And he, meanwhile, will be alone in the house with his ten billions, his ears permanently cocked for burglars. He will become suspicious, hard-hearted, and will look everyone over from top to toe. Aha, my friends, I thank God that our Salvatore has not found any wallet, which means that he will always be in need of money and his need will cause him to live at peace with his neighbour and love him so that he may be loved.'

'Professor, you've convinced me,' confessed Salvatore. 'From now on whenever I go out I shan't even watch where I put my feet for fear of finding ten billion lire!'

'Salvatore! Salvatore!' called Cazzaniga, putting his head round the door of the porter's lodge.

'Yes, Doctor,' replied the deputy-assistant porter, coming towards him.

'I need a favour, and you're the only person who can help me,' said Cazzaniga, looking a trifle sheepish. 'Two of my nephews are coming to Naples from Milan next Sunday to see the Inter match ... I don't like to bother you, but I know nothing about football and I haven't a clue where ...'

'Don't worry about it. Your Salvatore is here to solve all your problems. Tell me what it is you want.'

'As I was saying, these two nephews of mine have rung to ask me to get tickets for stand seats for the Napoli-Inter match, but I don't even know who sells them.'

'In actual fact, they're not on sale.'

'What do you mean?'

'Well, they are and they aren't. If you see what I mean.'

'I don't. Salvatore, I haven't got time for riddles this morning. It's nearly eight o'clock and I've got to get to the office. What I'd like to do is hand over the money for the tickets to you and ask you if you could possibly ...'

'Really, Doctor,' Salvatore interrupted, looking him squarely in the eyes, 'I don't understand you. Are you or are you not the chief personnel officer for Alfa Romeo? ... Then why do you get up at some unearthly hour every day to get to Pomigliano d'Arco on the dot? The one thing most people like about being departmental heads in a company is the possibility of getting up later; if it weren't for that, nobody would want the job. As Professor Bellavista's always saying, "Responsibility is nothing but a headache. Thank heaven that so many people are prepared to take it on instead of us!"'

'Forgive me, Salvatore, but I'm in a rush,' replied Cazzaniga, starting towards his car. 'Some other time I shall be delighted to discuss the motivation of a head of department, but all I'm asking now is that you do me the favour of getting hold of two tickets for the Napoli-Inter match.'

'That goes without saying,' said Salvatore reassuringly, running after him, 'but since the only person who can get them for us is a brother-cousin of mine who lives near Piazza Arenella, and as you have to go right past his door, I will, if you don't mind, hitch a lift, and then we can buy them this very morning.'

They got into the car, Cazzaniga switched on the ignition and waited, as instructed by the manual, for the engine to warm up.

'Congratulations, Doctor, what a beautiful car!' exclaimed Salvatore enthusiastically, looking around him. 'It's new, isn't it?'

'Yes, it's the new Alfa 75.'

'It's a beauty, and what a lot of dashboard lights! What's this one for, Doctor?' Salvatore was pointing to one of the control displays.

'That's the trip-computer.'

'The trip-computer? How about that!' exclaimed Salvatore admiringly. He went on, 'From what I've heard, a trip-computer means you don't have to worry about a thing, right?'

'Just about,' replied Cazzaniga shortly. He was evidently not disposed to be chatty first thing in the morning and was now starting to worry about the consequences of this trip with Salvatore.

Salvatore, however, was not so easily put off once his interest was engaged. 'But Doctor,' he insisted, 'what, in simple terms, does the trip-computer actually do?'

'It gives you information about the car's performance.'

'The performance?'

'Yes.'

'And then what?'

'Listen, Salvatore, what's the matter with you this morning?' grumbled Cazzaniga. 'What are you getting at? Do you want to buy an Alfa 75?'

'Good Lord, no! There's only one thing I want to know, and that is what happens if the trip-computer itself goes wrong. Does the car still work?'

'Yes.'

'So this trip-computer does nothing at all!'

'Listen,' Cazzaniga interrupted, 'I'd rather know if this ... brother ... cousin ...'

'Brother-cousin,' specified Salvatore.

'I don't know what a brother-cousin is,' Cazzaniga continued testily, 'but that's neither here nor there. Just tell me one thing: does this relative of yours live very far away from the ring-road?'

'No distance at all. His flat is just off Piazza Arenella. We can pop in, buy the tickets and be away in five minutes. I'd like you to meet him, he's a splendid chap. He was unemployed until a short while ago, then he got a job with the Napoli Football Club and now he's all set for a successful career.'

'So he's an employee of the Napoli club?'

'No, Doctor, he's not an employee! He's a ticket tout.'

'Ticket tout? But you said he was in a steady job!'

'Yes he is, because he's no longer a *volante*. The *bosses* took a liking to him and made him a *padroncino*, with his own *paranza*.'

'Forgive me, Salvatore, but I'm totally ignorant when it comes to football. What is a *volante*?'

'A *volante* is like a retailer, he sells tickets outside the stadium. A *padroncino* buys tickets wholesale and distributes them to the *volanti*. The *bosses* control the finances; they stay behind the lines, collect the money and risk losing a packet if a match is rained off.'

'How many people are involved in this?'

'About two thousand throughout Italy and they're nearly all Neapolitans.'

'Two thousand! Two thousand people selling tickets for Napoli matches?'

'No, not just that but for all kinds of events. If you were to go, say, to the Monza Grand Prix ... to Wimbledon for the Davis Cup ... to La Scala Milan ... or even to see Hamburg play Real Madrid in Germany, you could bet that any ticket tout you saw would be a Neapolitan.'

'And do they make a lot of money?'

'It's always a gamble. Sometimes they win, sometimes they lose,' replied Salvatore authoritatively and with a touch of admiration. 'They buy early, so they can't know whether it's going to rain or not. They take a personal risk much like an insurance company.'

'How do you mean?'

'Listen, and I'll explain it to you very carefully,' said Salvatore, speaking slowly and clearly as if Cazzaniga's was a case of retarded development. 'Forget Napoli which is a big club and doesn't need any extra help, but think instead of a small-town club in one of the minor leagues. In this case, if a *boss* buys 50 per cent of the tickets at a discount before the start of the season, he's taking a load off the minds of the members who can use the money advanced by the touts to plan their budget.'

'So they benefit the sport?'

'Of course. As I told you, they act like an insurance company that can make a gain or a loss depending on whether it rains or shines on the day of the match. And that's what it's all about.'

'Could I have two numbered stand seats?'

'They're fifty thousand lire each, so that's a hundred thousand for two,' replied Gaetaniello, nicknamed 'the student', in a businesslike tone of voice.

'A hundred thousand for two stand seats?!' exclaimed Cazzaniga.

'Sir,' explained the student, 'you are evidently not too well informed about current prices. A numbered seat, if you could find one for sale, would have cost the agent forty-five thousand lire; say he makes ten thousand lire, that's fifty-five thousand.

But as you are a friend of my cousin's, I've given you a special price. If you want to save money, I can offer you two corner tickets at eight thousand each.'

'No, thank you. It's just that a hundred thousand seemed a lot just to see a football match!'

'And you've been very lucky. These tickets only arrived from Milan this morning.'

'But there are no tickets left in Milan for the Napoli-Inter match,' Cazzaniga demurred naïvely.

'Naturally. We bought them all up, my colleague *Cape 'e chiuovo* and myself,' explained the student. 'To avoid disappointing our customers, we had to buy up a supply of tickets that had been allocated to the Inter fans.'

'Very well,' sighed Cazzaniga, taking a hundred thousand from his wallet. 'But you are sure, I presume, that these tickets are valid?'

'Doctor, those words should never have passed your lips,' protested the student, slightly offended. 'I forgive you because you're not a Neapolitan, but I would ask you to remember that I am selling from my own home. However, if you want references, no problem. You can make enquiries at the police station in Fuorigrotta, and they will tell you who I am.'

'Incidentally,' said Cazzaniga, 'aren't you ever worried about the police arresting you when you sell tickets outside the stadium?'

'The police are our allies. We often call them in ourselves.'

'You call in the police?!'

'Indeed we do,' confirmed the student, becoming quite heated. 'Our natural enemies are not the police but the forgers and the *azzeccatori*.[6] Forgers because they sell forged tickets and give the genuine touts a bad name, and the *azzeccatori* for much the same reasons. They all discredit us in the eyes of the general public. That's why we call the police and have them arrested as soon as we see them.'

'I see ... but who are the *azzeccatori*?' asked Cazzaniga, who

[6] Splicers.

was by now so intrigued with the business of ticket-touting that he had completely forgotten about his office.

'*Azzeccatori* are extremely cunning individuals who lurk just inside the gates. They relieve spectators of the torn half of the ticket, retrieve the other half, splice the two pieces quickly together and sell the reconstituted ticket outside the ground.'

Bellavista, Saverio, Salvatore and Capuozzo were gathered in the porter's lodge, Via Petrarca.

'Professor, do you remember that chap who said he was Maradona?' asked Saverio.

'Of course,' replied Bellavista. 'Did they get him?'

'No, but he's changed his job. He now organizes coach trips for fans who want to see the team play away. I met him yesterday in the Galleria. He gave me a publicity hand-out about the next match between Napoli and Firenze, look.'

Bellavista took the proffered leaflet and read aloud:

> FIORENTINA–NAPOLI CAROVANA AZZURRA
> with THE MARADONA BROTHERS
> Lire 49.500 – price includes:
> Admission to terrace
> Two-way journey in luxury coach
> Picnic lunch consisting of:
> 1 macaroni timbale
> 2 rice croquettes
> 1 bread roll
> 1 apple
> ½ bottle Peroncino
> 1 cup Borghetti coffee
> – A packet of Marlboro will be raffled
> during the journey

'Latter-day barbarians!' snorted Avvocato Capuozzo.

'What do you say, Professor?' asked Saverio. 'Shall we treat ourselves to a trip to Florence?'

'I confess to feeling very tempted, Savè,' the Professor replied with a smile, 'especially by the prospect of seeing a packet of Marlboro being raffled.'

'Then think no more about it, but come with us,' said Salvatore. 'I've already bought my ticket.'

'And I'm going with my uncle, Zio Nicola,' added Saverio. 'And thanks to him, if Napoli wins I get all my expenses reimbursed by the Vomero Over-Sixties Club.'

'Why's that?' enquired Bellavista. 'Why should they pay your expenses?'

'Because I'm taking Zì Nicola.'

'And who is Zio Nicola?'

'It's an old story,' replied Saverio. 'My uncle, you see, is well known for bringing good luck to Napoli. It just so happens that every time he has a pee Napoli scores a goal.'

'Oh, come on!' exclaimed the Professor with more than his usual scepticism. 'That must have been a mere coincidence.'

'No, Professor, you can't call this coincidence!' insisted Salvatore. 'This is a scientific fact, called "telekinesis"!'

'Scientific fact my eye!' sneered Capuozzo sarcastically, giving full rein to his scorn for Parthenopean football mythology. 'Perhaps we should send samples of Zio Nicola's urine to the laboratory for analysis!'

'Avvocà, you've never understood the first thing about football!' protested Saverio.

'And I'm proud of it...' declared Capuozzo.

'Say what you like, but the fact has been proved many times over,' asserted Saverio earnestly. 'The first manifestation of the phenomenon was in 1970, when the World Cup was being played in Mexico, do you remember? Well, Italy was playing Switzerland, and the match had only just started when Zì Nicola wanted to go to the bathroom. As he was peeing, Domenghini scored. That time, nobody took any notice. I remember just saying: "Zì Nicola, you missed a goal. Italy scored while you were in the bathroom..."'

'The goal was, of course, credited to Zì Nicola, not Domenghini,' remarked Capuozzo, more sarcastic than ever.

'The same thing happened without fail throughout the Italy-

Mexico game,' Saverio continued after shooting a withering glance at Capuozzo. 'Sixty-three minutes into the match – I'll never forget it as long as I live – it was actually me who said: "Zì Nicò, go and have a widdle, and I'll bet Italy scores like they did the other day!" Wowee! ... You lot won't believe it, but as soon as Zì Nicola went to the bathroom, Riva got a goal. Pandemonium broke loose! We were all hugging Zì Nicola while he was still peeing! And then there was that famous evening when Italy played Germany.'

'I was there too at the time: I can swear to it,' stated Salvatore, raising his hand like a witness taking the oath.

'We made Zì Nicola sleep all afternoon so he wouldn't sleep during the match. Just after the kick-off, I allowed him to go as he'd been dying for a pee for the last half-hour. And in fact, as if to prove me right, Zì Nicola hadn't even left the bathroom before Boninsegna put the ball in the net. One–nil to Italy. But at that very moment the Germans all crowded into our penalty area. It was like the siege of Fort Apache, the ball was whizzing backwards and forwards across the goal-mouth and Albertosi didn't know where to put himself to keep it out. I was keeping one eye on the TV and the other on my watch. I thought we'd done it, and then, into the last minute, that bastard Schnellinger popped up in front of our goal and scored the equalizer. They began extra time. Our late lamented friend, Signor Cantarelli, the accountant, who had already had two heart attacks at the time, said: "It's all over now, we've lost!" "Not a bit of it," I said, "We can't just surrender like that!" Now, while all this was going on, Zì Nicola had had plenty of time to refuel, especially since we'd made him drink two bottles of diuretic mineral water. Almost two hours had passed. We sent him to the bathroom. Now, Zì Nicola stands up ... Facchetti intercepts the ball ... Zì Nicola opens the bathroom door ... Rivera passes to Domenghine ...Zì Nicola lifts the seat ... Domenghini to Burgnich ... Zì Nicola starts to pee ... Burgnich scores!'

Saverio's radio-style commentary was interrupted by loud applause in which even Bellavista joined. The porter's lodge was now becoming ever more crowded with friends and the simply curious.

'Disgusting!' was Capuozzo's single, terse comment. It evoked no response at all.

'But that wasn't all,' said Saverio, beaming. 'Riva scored again, which made us three–two up. We were just about to toast an Italian victory when *chillu piezzo 'e mappina*[7] Müller scored an equalizer for Germany. Three–all. General despondency, Cantarelli faints, Salvatore and I carry Zì Nicola bodily into the bathroom. The poor old man's struggling for all he's worth but says that it's useless, that we're wasting our time and he just can't go, but we tell him: "Come on Zì Nicò, come on, just a drop," while someone runs the tap to stimulate him with the sound of running water and someone whispers "ssh, ssh, ssh, ssh", in his ear. At last, a tiny trickle appears. Boninsegna to Rivera, Rivera GOAL! Italy beat Germany four–three.'

The Maradona brothers' coach was not only far from luxurious but was a relic of the war, one of those dark blue coaches with plastic seats that had probably spent all its life plying between Naples and some little village buried deep in the Neapolitan hinterland. By way of compensation, however, it was rumoured that the picnic lunch would be excellent; it had been prepared by Signora Sorrentino, the mother of the Sorrentini brothers and famous for her macaroni timbales.

To everyone's surprise, the coach, instead of taking the Autostrada del Sole, headed up the Appian Way towards Cassino.

'Don't worry,' said the elder of the Sorrentino brothers. 'Because it's Sunday and the traffic is heavy, we're better off avoiding the autostrada to begin with. We'll stay on the Appian Way as far as Capua and join the autostrada there.' Then he turned to the driver, saying: '*Vamos muchacho, vamos.*' Pasquale Sorrentino apparently nourished a certain lingering nostalgia for his old job as Maradona's manager.

Anxious to gather first-hand information about Zì Nicola's

---

[7] That bit of a dishcloth.

amazing powers, Bellavista had seated himself next to the 'goal-maker' from the start. For the first few kilometres the old man dozed, lulled by the motion of the coach, but then, waking up with a jump and having completely forgotten why he was here, he turned to his nephew for enlightenment.

'Savè, Savè, where are we going?'

"O Zì, we're on our way to Florence, to see the match.'

'Match? What match?' replied Zì Nicola blankly.

'Fiorentina–Napoli.'

'*Gesù, Gesù*! Why do we have to go all the way to Florence to see a match? Can't we watch it on the telly?'

"O Zì, they're not showing it on the telly.'

'Tell me, Don Nicò,' said Professor Bellavista, 'are you a very keen Napoli fan?'

'*A me d'o Napoli nun me passa manco p'a capa!*'[8] stated Zì Nicola emphatically before putting his mouth to Bellavista's ear and asking, with a furtive look over his shoulder: 'Who are you? A journalist?'

'No.'

'Then I'll tell you what you should write in your paper,' said Zì Nicola, still in a whisper. 'That my Sundays have become murder. They allow me a pee first thing when I wake up, another at half past ten, and that's it. The bastards lock the toilet door. I can burst my bladder for all they care, but they won't let me pass another drop of water until the match starts, and sometimes I have to wait until well after the kick-off.'

'But why?' Bellavista asked, whispering too.

'The timing's decided by the trainer,' the old man replied with a jerk of his head in the direction of a red-headed fan.

'That's only logical: of course the expert has to decide such matters!' the latter responded. 'If our team isn't attacking at that moment, I can't afford to fire at random. The goal, as they say, has to develop.'

'How will you manage in Florence?'

'We've brought along everything necessary,' said the trainer

---

[8] 'I don't give a brass monkey for Napoli!'

with a glance at a large box at the back of the coach.

Suddenly the coach slowed down and then stopped as if it had run out of fuel. The driver tried the ignition a few times but without success. They were on a wide, sun-drenched road on the outskirts of Casaluce, a largish village not far from Aversa. After a cursory glance at the steaming engine, the ex-Maradona went to see if he could find a mechanic in the village. Time passed, everyone began looking at their watches. There was no sign of the former Maradona. A certain edginess began to diffuse itself through the ranks of the fans as all hope of ever reaching Florence faded progressively. The fake Argentinian reappeared, completely dispirited. Today being Sunday, not a single mechanic was to be found. One or two started to mutter about asking for their money back, but this threw the Sorrentino brothers into an immediate paroxysm of grief. Then Bellavista suggested a compromise solution: half their money back and a picnic meal here where they had stopped. The one ray of comfort amid the general gloom was that the coach had come to a halt right outside a lorry-drivers' trattoria, the 'Oasis'.

Everyone climbed out. The elder Sorrentino negotiated with the owner of the trattoria for the party to consume its own food on the premises. All they needed was wine, and this was ordered with alacrity, especially after the discovery of an excellent Gragnano, cooled in the bowels of the earth. Meanwhile, the proprietor offered the use of a radio so that they could follow the commentary in the sports programme. So, little by little, aided by the Gragnano, Signora Sorrentino's timbales and their own weariness, everyone became resigned to the change of programme.

The match began with Fiorentina on the attack. The party followed attentively, holding its breath whenever the ball was near Castellini's goal-mouth. At a certain point, Zì Nicola put his hand up, indicating that, as far as he was concerned, the moment had come. The trainer, however, disagreed. Some wanted an early lead. A heated debate broke out between those who wanted to play the Zì Nicola joker straight away and those who preferred to keep it in reserve. Suddenly, above the mêlée of voices, a shout was heard: 'All stay where you are. You are under arrest.'

Inspector Di Domenico and Sergeant Colapietro had got their hands on the Sorrentino brothers at last.

Everyone rose to their feet, some protesting and trying to defend the 'Maradona Brothers'. Di Domenico was unmoved.

'As I told you last time, Professor, if it were up to me I'd leave them alone, but they've gone too far,' puffed the Inspector, mopping his forehead with a large, pale blue handkerchief. 'This is the third bogus trip they've organized this year, and every time the coach stops in front of the same trattoria.'

The revelation caused an immediate alteration in the attitude towards the Sorrentino family: everyone clamoured for their money back. Zì Nicola, meanwhile, taking advantage of the confusion, slipped away to the toilet, but had hardly finished relieving himself before the radio commentator announced that Napoli had gone into the lead: Maradona had scored!

General rejoicing. Everyone hugged everyone else. Zì Nicola 'o Goleador was carried shoulder-high. The Inspector tried in vain to discover who had scored the goal. Colapietro threw his cap in the air as he had seen it done in American films. The proprietor of the 'Oasis' called for Gragnano all round, on the house. But as the toast was being drunk Di Domenico noticed that the Sorrentino brothers had vanished. Going outside, he found that the coach had also vanished.

'Colapiè, quick!' shouted the Inspector, dashing towards the car. 'Get in the other car and we'll give chase!'

'Inspector, a word with you, if I may,' yelled the proprietor of the 'Oasis', pelting after him. 'Don't spoil such a happy occasion: let them go. This is their final trip. Vincenzo Sorrentino's going straight from tomorrow. He's been offered a job by the Napoli Football Club as a stand-in for Maradona. They're going to use him to create a diversion when the team leaves the ground after training sessions.'

# The Landlord's Lament

'*Uè, uè, uè, uè, uè* ...' jeered the gang of little boys following Avvocato Capuozzo at a distance of a couple of metres.

The poor wretched man kept on walking, pretending to be unaware of his tormentors, but the little villains refused to let up. They were timing the jeers to his steps and at the same time making sounds very like 'raspberries' with their hands tucked under their bare armpits. This concordance of sounds known in Naples as *musica giapponese*, is very fashionable among certain elements of Neapolitan youth. For those who make a study of Parthenopean folk customs, the subscapular 'raspberry' is produced by placing a hand in the armpit and rhythmically raising and lowering the arm in such a way that air is compressed between the hollow of the hand and the body.

Capuozzo appeared quite indifferent to the teasing. In fact he was seething inside, but being determined not to give the rabble the satisfaction of knowing this, he had assumed an air of total absorption in his own thoughts.

'*Uè, uè, uè, uè, uè,*' his tormentors jeered persistently, ever closer to his heels. Each step provoked a *uè!* and a raspberry. The lawyer stopped for a second as if about to retrace his steps, then resumed walking, alternating a few fast steps with a few slower ones in an attempt to escape the obsessive rhythm of the jeers, but the boys' expertise was diabolical and the only result of the sudden pause was a prolonged salvo of 'raspberries'.

'*Uè, uè, uè, uè, uè!*'

Don Ferdinando, the assistant porter, watched the scene from his accustomed chair outside the main door and shouted threateningly at the small delinquents.

'Stop that at once, I tell you! One of these days I shall get up and beat the living daylights out of the lot of you!'

Capuozzo, knowing better than to count on help from the assistant porter, opted for the only available refuge from the attentions of the rabble: the porter's lodge. The boys hung around for a while, continuing the performance.

'Hear that?' asked Capuozzo of all present. 'And what's to blame for it? The fair-rent system.'

'Avvocà,' responded Salvatore, 'how can you possibly blame the fair-rent system! If the boys tease you, it's because they think you're a bit odd. What do they know about the fair-rent system? They're as innocent as babes!'

'Innocent as babes indeed!' retorted Capuozzo. 'Salvatò, if the boys tease me it's because the government has reduced the status of the landlord to that of a puppet. There was a time when things were different, when the landlord was a power to be feared. His tenants scattered at his approach and ran to warn the others with cries of "Watch out, watch out! The landlord's coming!" Some people even disguised themselves so that he wouldn't recognize them. But nowadays they add insult to injury and even the children mock him! Hear that mob outside? Well, they're the tenants of the future!'

'There's one thing I don't understand, Avvocato,' said Bellavista. 'Are you complaining because respect for the landlord has declined or because the fair-rent system has resulted in rents that are too low?'

'Both. And the one is a consequence of the other. I went to see a tenant of mine this morning, a man called Luigi Improta who runs a shoe-repair business in Via Sergente Maggiore. Seeing that we're already half-way through the month and that he was two weeks in arrears, I asked him politely for the rent. And do you know what he said? Nothing, absolutely nothing, as if I hadn't opened my mouth! Then, instead of making any attempt at an excuse or explanation such as, for instance, a lapse of memory, he turned to his brother and said: "Gennaro, have you got some change for Capuozzo?" Those were his precise words: "Have you got some change for Capuozzo," just as if I were a beggar asking for alms. And what could I say? Nothing. He was right. Sixty thousand lire a month for a corner shop in Via Sergente Maggiore is effectively a beggar's pittance. You might point out that there is a legal right of eviction from commercial premises and ask me why I don't invoke it. I can't, because he would maintain that the *basso* is a dwelling, not a shop. But, you say, how can it be a dwelling if the Council itself has stuck a notice on it saying "Groundfloor premises unsuitable for residential use"? Improta snaps his fingers at the notice and lives there just the same. But, you object, haven't you just said that he carries on a shoe-repair business there? Yes, but he will argue that repairing shoes is his hobby. See where we've got to now? To the point where a grubby illiterate who was, until recently, nicknamed "pigsfoot", has learnt the word "hobby"! When his younger brother gave me the sixty thousand lire, he took the notes, all filthy, from the pocket of his trousers and put them into my hand one at a time for all the world as though he were performing an act of charity!'

'Tell me, Avvocato, how many *bassi* and blocks of flats do you own scattered throughout Naples?' asked Salvatore out of curiosity.

'What's that got to do with lack of respect?' retorted Capuozzo, slightly taken aback.

'Nothing, I was just wondering,' said Salvatore. 'Because if you own as many as people think you do, then even if they're all rent-controlled, I reckon you find yourself with so much money by the end of the month that not even you know what to do with it all! Besides, unless I'm mistaken, you're a bachelor so you don't even have to support a family!'

'What do you think you're talking about!' protested Capuozzo, turning rather redder than usual. 'How much property do I own?! How much money do I make?! Am I or am I not a bachelor?! Forgive me, but it's none of your business!'

'I asked because this is a democratic society. And anyway, what harm is there in asking these questions? I only enquired out of curiosity, not to check up on your tax liability,' said Salvatore defensively.

'Salvatore,' retorted the lawyer, 'you're confusing democracy and bad manners!'

'Now, now,' said Saverio cajolingly, 'don't get so worked up, Avvocà. You know how it is with Salvatore: he's always had a slight leaning towards communism. He's convinced that all property is theft, and since you own so much property...'

'Ah, which I'm supposed to have stolen from one of you?' snapped Capuozzo. 'Clearly, the fact that I own property means that my ancestors, unlike yours, worked for generations to amass an inheritance.'

'And then you came along and that was that,' concluded Salvatore affably.

'What do you mean, that was that?' asked Capuozzo. 'I don't practise in court, but I work from morning till night all the same, managing the property, and God alone knows what an effort that is and how much lip I have to put up with!'

'Avvocà, you allow yourself to be rattled rather too easily,' remarked Bellavista. 'As we all know, Salvatore is a card-carrying member of the Communist party, and Karl Marx did say that every great fortune has been founded by a brigand.'

'Very well, this is the point at which I leave you,' said Capuozzo, rising and making for the glass door. 'Since even a man of letters like Professor Bellavista chooses to indulge in cheap demogogy, I have nothing more to say. The thing that I find most surprising is that while even the Russians and Chinese have observed that Communism is in crisis, the views discussed in this porter's lodge have remained unchanged since '68.'

'Is Capuozzo right in saying that Communism is in crisis even in Russia?' asked Salvatore, considerably disturbed.

'All the great systems of political economy are in crisis,' replied Bellavista. 'That goes for both Communism and capitalism alike. The problem for economists today is to find a middle way between the two systems.'

'Tell me something, Professor,' intervened Saverio. 'If Karl Marx invented Communism, who invented Capitalism?'

'Ah, if we had to name a single founding father of Capitalism, it would probably be Adam Smith, a Scotsman who lived a couple of hundred years ago and wrote a book called *Inquiry into the Nature and Causes of the Wealth of Nations*. But to be honest, I'm afraid that Capitalism probably invented itself and Smith only documented its history. However, just to put the discussion on a firm footing, this is what happened. Smith stated that the more a man works, the more wealth he produces. Everything that he produces over and above his own capacity for consumption adds to the wealth of his country. But how can men be persuaded to produce more than they really need? That is the problem.'

'But Communism also holds that wealth equals work,' objected Salvatore. 'Only the wealth hardly ever goes into the pockets of the workers.'

'Yes, but Smith's reasoning was much more subtle,' continued Bellavista. 'Let's see what he said. In order to persuade a man to produce more than he can consume, we must rely totally on his competitive instinct. Smith would say to him, "If you work hard, I will reward this work with lots of pieces of paper on which I shall write one pound sterling, a hundred pounds sterling or a thousand pounds sterling, and the more of these that you can amass, the happier you will be. In practice, Capitalism relies on human selfishness and greed.'

'I don't think much of that,' commented Salvatore.

'Karl Marx, on the other hand,' continued the Professor, 'having learnt from Jean Jacques Rousseau that man was naturally good, decided to base himself on this goodness. In other words, it was as if he had said to our man: You must work for the collective good, then everything you produce will be divided equally among the citizens of your country. Seventy years after the first experiments with Communism, we have done our sums and come to the conclusion that Capitalism understood the human heart rather better than Communism. Man is not as good as Rousseau imagined. He was prepared to work really hard in countries where labour was rewarded by money, but idled in those where he was treated as a mere hireling.'

'So I was right!' crowed Saverio. 'Capitalism is the better system!'

'Wait. Let's analyse the problem rather more closely,' replied Bellavista. 'In its reliance on egoism and competition, Capitalism has come to regard money as an end in itself and not just a means of acquiring goods. Practically speaking, men, by watering the plantlets of their egoism day by day, have ended up by transforming these plantlets into a lethal jungle. The worship of Money has sanctified the grossest crimes, the race for Power has corrupted men's souls, and I'm not only thinking of the really big Mafia-style gangsters but also of the surgeon who performs a caesarean when it is not strictly necessary, the tax inspector who accepts a bribe, the farmer who burns down a wood to gain extra grazing land, and so on . . .'

'. . . and so, as I've always said, Communism is the better system,' said Salvatore, preening himself.

'Hold on,' said Bellavista warningly. 'Let's see what happened in the meantime on the other side. After Marx came Lenin, and after Lenin Joseph Stalin. Now, as far as one can tell, Stalin was rather less idealistic than his predecessors; one might even say heavy-handed as well. When he saw that agriculture was failing to meet the quotas he demanded, he summoned his farmers and told them that if they weren't going to work for love of their fellow-citizens, then they would work by constraint. Final result: more equality maybe, but less freedom.'

'So,' concluded Saverio, 'if I've understood what you're saying, you're neither a capitalist nor a Marxist.'

'Quite correct.'

'So what are you?'

'Perhaps I should call myself a Popperian optimist.'

'Good grief!' exclaimed Saverio. 'What's that? A new political party?'

'Quite the opposite,' replied Bellavista. 'It simply means a way of looking at things based on the theories of a great philosopher, Karl Popper.'

'Professor, if these theories are complicated, it's no use your trying to explain them. We'll take your word for it,' said Saverio. 'But if you think that we're capable of understanding them, go ahead, because for myself, I must confess, I would rather like to be able to say one day that I too am a Popperian.'

'Popper was convinced that one can learn from one's mistakes,' said Bellavista, warming to his subject. 'And he was right, because if you analyse a mistake in all good faith, it becomes a step forward towards the truth. Popper's advice was to treat with caution everyone who proposes happiness as the ultimate goal and rely instead on those who propose small improvements to be carried out step by step.'

'I wouldn't dream of contradicting you, Professor,' said Salvatore, 'but to me that seems no more than a form of words. What did Popper actually suggest we should do to improve the conditions around us such as unemployment, the level of crime, the danger of nuclear war and all that jazz?'

'Popper believed in words and, to be more precise, in communication between liberal-minded men. Liberal-mindedness is fundamental to Popper's thinking. The old philosopher said that in order to arrive at the Truth, it is essential that all parties to the discussion be prepared to modify their own views if and when they are proved to be wrong.'

'Forgive me, Professor,' exclaimed Saverio, 'but your Popper doesn't seem to me to be saying anything very important. It's only logical to change one's mind when someone else can prove we're wrong!'

'Not always. Most men, when they're involved in an argument, are unable to reason logically and will maintain that they are the only repositories of the Truth, refusing to listen to what the other side is saying. Sometimes, indeed, they end up by becoming even more radical than they were to begin with and even further away from the other man's point of view.'

'Maybe, but where does all this get us?'

'It teaches us to beware of revolutionaries and to prefer reformers. Popper says that the fight against poverty must be conducted by the Government, while the search for happiness should be left to private enterprise. In other words, we need socialists at the top and entrepreneurs at the bottom.'

'Why do you call yourself an optimist?' asked Saverio.

'Because I am convinced that the world is improving every day.'

'What an extraordinary thing to say, Professor!' exclaimed Salvatore. 'The world's crawling with evildoers, thieves, murderers, terrorists, yet you say it's improving?!'

'Criminals only seem to be numerous because we hear so much about them,' replied the Professor. 'There actually used to be more of them, but no one knew about it. Remember, until only a couple of hundred years ago, no one would dare go out into the streets without a sword. But if you think about it, nothing bad happens in the world without it being reported in the papers and on radio and television. But despite what we read in the papers, I still believe that humanity is improving daily, by which I mean that the average quality of the human race is constantly improving. This is vitally important, because only people of a better quality can provide the basis for the development of a better society. I'll give you an example. Think of a corrupt, dishonest man....'

'Don Carmine Silipo, my landlord,' suggested Saverio.

'... Well, this man will still be corrupt and dishonest after a revolution.'

'So what should we do?'

'Take a long-term view,' replied Bellavista. 'Popper maintains that a process of reform is the only way to encourage a slow but sure increase in the quality of the average man. Such a process of reform would ensure that the son of the corrupt man would certainly be better than his father.'

'It's a possibility,' murmured Salvatore doubtfully. 'But I suspect that if we were to propose Popper as an election candidate we'd poll fewer votes than any other party, and while you can be many things in politics, revolutionary, reformist or what you will, one thing you can't be is few in numbers, or the majority will simply trample you – and Popper – into the dust!'

'Salvatore's outside,' said Signora Cazzaniga.

'Tell him to come in,' replied her husband.

It was a Saturday morning, and Dr Cazzaniga was in his study working on his tax returns. As a director of Alfa Romeo, he had no fiscal obligations at this time of year, which was November, but as the proprietor of two small apartments in Milan, he was required to deal with the paperwork.

'May I come in?' asked Salvatore, standing in the doorway.

'Please do, and thanks for coming,' said Cazzaniga. 'I asked you to come up because I wanted to ask you a big favour...'

'At your service. You only have to ask and it shall be done.'

'Please sit down.'

'No thank you, Doctor, I speak better on my feet.'

'Well, as I was saying, I need your help. My brother Umberto is to be the new manager of the Naples branch of IBM Italia...'

'My warmest congratulations.'

'... and is to be transferred here to Naples on the first of January. Now, since the IBM offices are also in Via Orazio, we simply must find him a flat in this part of town.'

'That won't be easy, Dottò,' replied Salvatore with the authority of a professional. 'Without the help of a particular stroke of luck, there's not a corner to be had in the whole of Posillipo.'

'And what form would this stroke of luck take?'

'The death of Signora Schilizzi. We've all been expecting it for the last five months, especially me and my wife Rachelina.'

'How do you mean?'

'It's like this. Signora Schilizzi, poor woman, is terminally ill. She's going to die. She's lived in this block for over twenty years, third floor, entrance B, rent controlled. The lady doesn't get on with her son; she's tight-fisted and keeps him short of the readies. One day she bought herself a colour television. Believe me, Dottò, it's a beauty! Twenty-seven-inch anti-glare screen, and ninety-nine channels! I helped the man from the shop take it upstairs. As soon as Sasà saw us carrying the box into the flat, he went absolutely wild. "I don't believe it!" he said to his mother. "You spend all that money on a new television set, yet you refused to buy me an Armani overcoat!" To which the lady replied: "If you don't like the television, I shall leave it to Salvatore when I die." And that's why I've hung on to my black and white. The doctor looking after her said that she will certainly die before the end of the year.'

'I see,' said Cazzaniga. 'But apart from the fact that I wish the lady as long a life as possible, her son would presumably take over the flat.'

'Not at all,' replied Salvatore. 'He has always said that he doesn't like living in Naples and wants to move to Milan or Turin.' He lowered his voice conspiratorially and continued: 'The reason is, you see, that Sasà has slight homosexual tendencies and here in Naples we don't treat such people with sufficient respect. We call them *ricchioni*[1]. That offends the young man so much that he gets hysterical. But in the North they call them gays, and he likes that better. Now, in return for a small sum of money, Sasà would give us an option on the flat. He could buy himself the Armani overcoat and we could get him to sign a document promising to let us have the flat as soon as his mother dies.'

'That sounds most impractical,' objected Cazzaniga, rather shocked. 'And I must admit that I find the business of basing one's hopes on the death of the poor woman morally reprehensible. And what if she doesn't die?'

'She's going to die sooner or later, it's only a matter of months. It's the World Cup next year, and I've got to see that in colour!'

'No, Salvatore, forget about Signora Schilizzi's flat. I don't want anything to do with it. How could I explain to my brother that our hopes depend on the death of a sickly old lady?'

'Your choice. I suggested it because it could have meant you both living in the same building some day.'

'Thank you, but I repeat that it doesn't seem very practical,' reiterated Cazzaniga. 'For one thing, what excuse would we give the lady for wanting to view her flat?'

'There is another possibility.'

'What's that?'

'A flat belonging to Baron Belisario.'

'Tell me more.'

---

[1] *Ricchioni*: Slang, the equivalent of 'poofters'.

'I've heard the Baron recently got permission to evict a tenant for being consistently in arrears. The building's a bit old, but in a nice area. It's on the hill going down to Arco Mirelli, almost in Riviera di Chiaia, less than a kilometre away from IBM.'

'So let's not waste any time. Give him a ring.'

'It's best to go and see him. He'll hear from your accent that you're Milanese and that will make a good impression.'

'Where does he live?'

'At this time of day the Baron will be sunning himself on the terrace of the Circolo Canottieri Napoli.[2] If we go now, he's bound to offer us an apéritif.'

'Fine, but the only drawback is that I haven't got the car today, it's being serviced.'

'That doesn't matter,' replied Salvatore, 'we can take the 140 and get off at Santa Lucia; the Club's only a couple of minutes' walk from there.'

As was his wont on every fine day, Emanuele Belisario, Baron Airola and Altavilla, known to his friends as 'Bel Ami', was stretched out in the sunshine on the Circolo Napoli terrace while Cenzino, his manservant, read him the daily newspaper. The Baron, wearing a tweed suit and brown Church's shoes, lay in a deckchair provided with a footrest, his eyes closed as he savoured the tepid November sun. Cenzino, liveried in white, stood at his side reading out the headlines in *Il Mattino*.

'Craxi and De Mita: Agreement imminent between Socialists and Christian Democrats.'

'Not interested. Next one,' ordered the recumbent Baron without opening his eyes or moving a millimetre.

'Trade-gap widens: fifty billion more than forecast,' Cenzino continued in a monotone.

'Not interested. Next one,' repeated the Baron.

'Big Feminist Demonstration in Africa.'

'Feminists must decide what they want, equality or happi-

[2] Naples Rowing Club.

ness,' pronounced Bel Ami. 'However, I'm not interested. Next one.'

'Treasury minister declares war on tax-dodgers.'

'Has he imposed the death penalty?' asked the Baron, opening one eye and fixing it upon Cenzino.

'No.'

'Then I'm not interested. Next one!'

Antonio, the aged steward of the Club, approached the Baron. Bending towards him, he said:

'Barò, there are two gentlemen asking for you.'

Out of the corner of his eye, Baron Airola and Altavilla saw the slightly rotund figure of Salvatore and that of a man he did not know at the far end of the terrace.

'Ask them to come over.'

Followed by Cazzaniga, Salvatore approached, smiling, while Antonio and Cenzino moved a couple of cane chairs nearer the baron's deckchair.

'Barò,' began Salvatore, 'may I have the honour of presenting Dr Cazzaniga, managing director of Alfa Romeo ...'

'Just a moment, I'm not the managing director, only the chief personnel officer at Pomigliano,' said Cazzaniga, correcting him.

'Yes, but he comes from Milan,' said Salvatore, clarifying the matter.

'It's a pleasure. Belisario,' replied the Baron, rising.

'The pleasure's mine.'

'Make yourself comfortable. Splendid weather today,' said the Baron, glancing at the sky and then resuming his recumbent posture on the deckchair. 'One could even get out on the water if one was so inclined. Can I offer you a drink? Campari? An apéritif? I would recommend a copacabana.'

'A copacabana suits me fine,' replied Salvatore rather cheekily and without the slightest idea what a copacabana might be.

'I'd prefer a coffee, if I may,' murmured Cazzaniga.

'So, Cenzì,' said the Baron, 'ask them to bring two copacabanas and one coffee. We'll continue reading the paper later: don't lose the place.' He then turned to Cazzaniga, saying:

'I dislike handling the paper myself, so I get Cenzino to read it to me. The print is so dirty.'

'You're quite right, Barò,' echoed Salvatore. 'The print is dirty. Reporters write nothing but muck.'

'So tell me, to what do I owe the honour?' asked the Baron.

'Barò,' began Salvatore, 'forgive us for disturbing you, but the doctor's brother, who is to be the new managing director of IBM, is moving to Naples, so . . .'

'He's only a branch manager,' Cazzaniga corrected him. 'I cannot understand why Salvatore always exaggerates professional titles.'

'Pay no attention. It's a Neapolitan custom,' replied the Baron indulgently.

'So, as I was saying,' continued Salvatore, 'Doctor Cazzaniga's brother is being transferred to Naples and as I know that you've just evicted that tenant of yours from Arco Mirelli, I took the liberty . . .'

'I only wish to God I had evicted him!' exclaimed the Baron. 'Not even a bomb would shift that chap!'

'But didn't you win the case?'

'Indeed I did. But it's one thing to win a case, and quite another to shift a tenant! All evictions in Naples are interdicted until further orders and in the meantime that bastard goes on paying me half the rent.'

'How do you mean, half the rent?' asked Cazzaniga.

'I'll explain. He claims that my father let him have the flat before the war for half the normal rent because it was inhabited by *'o munaciello* and no one else would live there.'

'The little monk?' repeated Cazzaniga with an enquiring glance at Salvatore.

'Yes. According to the tenant, my father and his grandfather had an agreement between them the purpose of which was to disprove all the rumours. If I'm to believe my father, Eduardo[3] got the idea for *Questi fantasmi* from this very case. Have you seen the play?'

---

3 Eduardo De Filippis.

'No.'

'Well, to put the matter in a nutshell, my tenant refuses to pay more than half the rent because he says I must claim the other half from *'o munaciello*.'

'And you can't do a thing about it?' asked Salvatore.

'What more can I do? Win another lawsuit?' replied the Baron, opening his arms in a gesture of resignation. 'Last year I tried to frighten him by sending him a notification, by recorded delivery, of my intention to sell the property, and sent along a fake prospective purchaser, a friend of mine. First he welcomed him, then told him not to go into the living room because that was *'o munaciello*'s favourite place. The room was in total darkness, but my friend insisted on going in all the same. And what happened? He had hardly put a foot inside the door before he got a couple of hefty slaps in the face and a kick up the backside.'

'Did he have an accomplice concealed in the living room?' asked Cazzaniga, considerably startled.

'Either that or *'o munaciello* really was there,'' remarked Salvatore.

'Here are our copacabanas,' said the Baron.

'But who is this *munaciello*?' asked Cazzaniga.

'A phantom monk,' replied Salvatore. 'There are hundreds of families in Naples who are quite used to the idea and live perfectly happily with a *munaciello* in their home.'

There was standing room only on the 140, and the best Cazzaniga and Salvatore could do was hold on to the rail behind the driver's seat.

'Do you believe in ghosts?' asked Cazzaniga, resuming the discussion.

'No, not in ghosts as such, but I do believe in *'o munaciello*. You see, Dottò, *'o munaciello* is a child-phantom and, like all children, he's always ready for a game. Haven't you ever had a morning when everything seems to slip out of your hands? That's *'o munaciello*, who just keeps nudging you because he happens to be in a playful mood. Or maybe, some other day, you drop a pen, say, and when you bend down to pick it up it's vanished. "Strange," you say, "it fell just here." Then you look further and find it under the sofa. You make nothing of it at the time, but you should have asked yourself how on earth it got under the sofa. A pen doesn't walk! No, but the explanation is simple. It was *'o munaciello*: he kicked it there.'

'It must be quite dreadful to live with a *munaciello*, always supposing they exist,' remarked Cazzaniga.

'Not necessarily,' replied Salvatore. 'If *'o munaciello* takes a liking to you, your fortune's made. You find yourself winning lottery prizes, having hunches, inspirations. He looks after you like a guardian angel. And on top of all that he'll protect your home from thieves and any other mischief-maker. Because what you mustn't forget is that *'o munaciello* develops an attachment for the house itself. Anyone who enters it without his permission had better look out! You're better off with a *munaciello* than a burglar alarm.'

'Excuse me,' said the bus driver to Salvatore, interrupting him, 'but do you often use this route?'

'No, why do you ask?'

'Do you know whether I should go straight on to Via Domenico Morelli or turn left into Via Arcoleo? You see, I'm standing in for a colleague who was taken ill at the last minute, and as I was told to leave at once because the bus was late already, I didn't even have time to check the route.'

'You have to turn down Via Arcoleo,' said a short, dumpy little man, pushing himself forward between Salvatore and Cazzaniga, 'then you go round Piazza Vittoria and towards Riviera di Chiaia.'

'That's all wrong!' intervened a woman with three small children clutching at her skirts. 'You go down Via Domenico Morelli, take the second turning on the left, then Via Gaetani and on to Riviera di Chiaia without touching Piazza Vittoria.'

With such contradictory advice being offered, the driver elected to stop. The cars blocked behind the bus set up a din of protest.

'My dear lady, don't talk nonsense!' retorted the short gentleman. 'The 140 used to go along Via Gaetani thirty years ago, then they re-routed it down Via Arcoleo to avoid congestion.'

'No, you're quite wrong there,' intervened an elderly gentleman. 'Thirty years ago Via Gaetani was one-way in the opposite direction, but now it's one-way from this direction as the lady said.'

'What is the point of all that!' shouted the short gentleman. 'The direction indicated by the lady is quite immaterial! I know the route of the 140 and I'm telling you it goes down Via Arcoleo!'

'You think you know better than me although I *live* in Via Gaetani?' protested the woman bitterly. 'If you don't believe me, I'll show you the route-plan at the bus stop!'

'Now,' intervened a man dressed in mechanic's overalls, 'seeing that the lady wishes to get off in Via Gaetani, right outside her own door, we must re-route one of the City buses, I suppose.'

'So why not! She's got three small children with her, poor thing!' said a woman of humble appearance. 'Do her a favour and go down Via Gaetani!'

'And leave me to walk all the way to Via Arcoleo?' retorted the short gentleman indignantly.

'Go down Via Gaetani, I tell you!' yelled the lady to the driver.

'Dottò,' remarked Salvatore, 'you are witnessing the hijacking of a city bus.'

'Listen,' shouted the driver to his passengers, quitting his seat behind the wheel, 'seeing that you cannot agree, I'm going to walk to the next stop and look at the route-map. I'll be back in a tick: don't move.'

He clambered out of the bus and, having walked about ten metres, encountered a policeman. The latter's gestures plainly indicated that he too was unsure about the 140's route, and indeed both of them set off to ask directions at the paper shop in Via Arcoleo.

'Salvatore,' said Cazzaniga, considerably discouraged, 'I'm afraid my brother isn't going to enjoy living in Naples very much. He's not like me, you see. He likes things to be just so ...

he won't compromise ... he works for IBM. I'm very fond of this city of yours, but I don't think he'll ever adapt. What with *'o munaciello* ... bus drivers who don't know the route ... here time has stood still. Whether it's a good thing or a bad thing I wouldn't know, but my brother is not the sort of person to cope with it.'

# *Socrates and Television*

SOCRATES Let's rest beneath this cedar and discuss the question whether, with the passage of time, men are becoming better than their fathers or not.

CRITO I wouldn't like to be thought a pessimist like Antisthenes, but I fear that the modern generation lacks the qualities we normally associate with people of good sense and which are indispensable to the philosopher.

SOCRATES My good Crito, can you support your statement with an example?

CRITO Unhappily, I can find such an example in the very bosom of my own family. I refer, as you have probably guessed already, to my son Thrasibulus. Instead of applying himself to the reading of good books and the study of nature, the boy sleeps a good part of the day and spends the night in a dive in Athens called the Dionysus Night Club.

SOCRATES Whereas when you were a boy, Crito, you read and studied all day long? Because this is the crux of the argument. Only by comparing the virtues and vices of the modern generation with the virtues and vices that we old ones had at their age can we judge whether humanity is getting better or worse.

CRITO I'm afraid I should have to say no to your question, Socrates. When we were young, we too used to spend our nights out on the town: I used to walk with you to the deme of Alopece and you walked me back to the Ceramicus. But, thanks be to the Gods, we talked, and it was this constant discussion that formed our minds and our souls. But what can the youth of today expect to learn shut up every evening in a dark and smoky disco where the most one can do is order a drink in sign-language?

SOCRATES But why do they refuse to talk?

CRITO They couldn't even if they wanted to. The music is so loud that all verbal communication is impossible. You will remember how we ourselves used to dance the *kordax* and the *sikinnis* by moonlight when we were boys, but between the dances we rested and got to know one another. But today the fashion is all for disco-music, a noise inspired by no Muse at all, that blares out non-stop and to which they dance each one on his or her own, sunk in heaven knows what gloomy thoughts. That's why I call the sons degenerate, and when I call them degenerate I am not thinking only of my own family but also of the sons of Aristides, Thucidides, Cimon and Pericles and comparing them with their fathers.

SOCRATES Permit me to doubt the truth of that, O Crito. Even Themistocles, and Hesiod before him, and Homer before him, complained about the youth of their day. Judging from their accounts, every generation has been worse than the foregoing one. But if that were really so, our own sons would be monsters, more ferocious than the Erinnyes and the Furies put together. I have a suspicion that whenever we recall the days of our own youth, a kindly demon lurking in our minds wipes away all recollection of the bad things and allows only the Good and Sublime to resurface. We only have to remind ourselves of Thyestes feeding his brother on the flesh of his own young nephews, of Hercules killing Telamon just because he had preceded him through the gates of Ilium, and of the twins

Proetus and Acrissius fighting for their own selfish interests while still in their mother's womb waiting to be born, to lose a little of our confidence in the idea that the past was better than the present.

CRITO You are probably right, O Socrates, but heed the words of a friend who loves you and take comfort if the stranger you encounter in the streets by night is a man of our own age, but be on your guard if he happens to be an Athenian youth.

SOCRATES My dear Crito, look! Here comes Simmias the Theban. Let's ask him if the young men of Thebes are also intent on nothing but pleasure and idleness.

CRITO Dear Simmias, come and sit here beside us on the grass and join in our discussion. Socrates and I were talking about the mores of the modern generation. From what you have seen, would you consider the youths in Boethia to be better or worse than their fathers before them?

SIMMIAS I really don't know what to say, my dear Crito. I do not think a great deal of either. All I ever see in Thebes is men and women sitting silently in front of television sets. We've got to the point now where 'Boethians' and 'television addicts' are practically synonymous throughout Greece.

SOCRATES Comfort yourself, O Crito, with the thought that in Athens, too, most adult people shut themselves up at home to watch television. And, what is worse, Athenians sometimes switch on the television even when they have no desire to watch it. The other evening I was a guest of Callias, and I noticed that the television remained switched on throughout the meal even though no one was paying any attention to it. I couldn't resist asking my host if the box were a kind of lantern that he should switch it on every evening as soon as he set foot in the house.

CRITO I suspect your bitter words about television, O

Socrates, derive from the fact that it was the cause of a quarrel between you and Xanthippe. Critias the son of Callaeschrus told me that last week, while the poor lady was watching a play by Aristophanes, you smashed the screen by throwing a stone at it. The following day everyone in the agora was saying that given half a chance you would have thrown the stone at the writer himself.

SOCRATES That is not a correct account of the course of events, O Crito. Xanthippe was watching a television play by Aristophanes when the door opened and in walked Callicles, that second-rate Sophist I once humiliated in front of the whole Prytaneum. Callicles's face was bloated, his nose was purple and he was clutching a stone. He was obviously the worse for drink. I asked him what he wanted at that hour of the night and he replied: "Just for once, I want you to admit that I'm right. And if you don't admit that I'm right within one second, I'll smash your television!" What was I, a weak old man, expected to do when confronted by a raving madman? I looked at the set and saw they were showing the two hundred and twenty-second part of this Aristophanes serial and replied: "I am convinced you're wrong, O Callicles," and he threw the stone. Then, to calm him down, I said, "Now go on your way with joy, for this evening, for the first time in your life, you just may have been right."'

CRITO If you didn't throw the stone yourself, Socrates, the effect was just the same as if you had, but instead of your smashing Xanthippe's television, Callicles did it for you. When Simmias was talking just now about the Boethians spending all their time watching television, I saw a look in your eyes that suggested you would like to throw a million stones! Tell me honestly if I have truly divined your thoughts.

SOCRATES You are mistaken, my good old Crito. I have no quarrel with television as such, indeed quite the contrary. I value the news bulletins and every programme that allows me to see the world without being obliged to be continually packing and unpacking a suitcase. I only object to the use to which the medium of television is put by the state and the independent companies alike. They show nothing but a succession of futile, repetitive programmes, quizzes, soap operas and trashy shows. It's like being asked to a banquet and then being given dessert for starters, dessert for main course, dessert instead of fruit and dessert for dessert.

CRITO Why do you not speak to them and persuade them to alter their programme policy?

SOCRATES I tried but it was a waste of breath. One of the archons wanted control over state broadcasting and the other was protecting the interests of private companies. The former accorded the latter special privileges in a decree and in return obtained greater influence over the state channels, but neither of them consulted the interests of the Athenian public.

SIMMIAS If you had the power, how would you use television, O Socrates?

SOCRATES The first thing I would do would be to drop the test card.

SIMMIAS The test card?

SOCRATES Yes. I would replace it with an educational programme costing virtually nothing.

SIMMIAS Please explain.

SOCRATES You see, Simmias, here in Athens we have a big problem. The criminal population is swelling visibly and our prisons can no longer cope with the numbers. To make room for new criminals, old ones are frequently paroled, and there's an amnesty every four or five years which is damaging for public morale.

SIMMIAS But how can television help to solve this problem?

SOCRATES Wait a moment and I'll tell you. Listen to this story about Solon the great lawgiver.

SIMMIAS I am listening, O Socrates.

SOCRATES A thief once broke into the house of an old, blind man and stole everything he had. But someone saw him leaving the house he had robbed and the day after he was brought in chains before Solon who said, in his wisdom: "If I sent you to prison I should be doing you a favour by helping you to hide your shame. I think it preferable that you be put on public exhibition, for only thus will you be brought to realize what other people think of your action." And he had him hung up in a cage between the columns of the Temple of Zeus.

SIMMIAS I still cannot grasp the logic of your argument, O Socrates.

SOCRATES Be more patient, O Simmias, and you will understand. On the day he gave that judgement, Solon invented the pillory. He realized that to expose a criminal in public could be a more educative punishment than a few years in prison. Now, since there is no agora vast enough to hold all the citizens of the state, I am proposing that we should adopt the medium of television, the televisual piazza, as it were, in its place, and expose the criminal's head instead of the test card which serves no useful purpose at all.

CRITO Do you think it would shame the guilty?

SOCRATES Indeed I do, especially if their crime were described in every last detail. I'll give you an example. The Tax Inspectorate discovers, following investigations, that Erissimachus the surgeon has declared a much lower income than the one he has actually received. His sentence is seven days' exposure on the screen coupled with the following text: "This is Erissimachus, son of Acumenus, guilty of tax evasion, a surgeon who habitually earns two million minae for performing a simple appendectomy yet has never declared a monthly income in excess of one and a half million minae." Or take another case, that of two men arrested for mugging an old woman. The tribunal sentences them to two months' tele-exposure. Every evening, when people switch on their sets, they see one of the two villains with his head in a pillory and a subtitle that reads: "A particularly nasty individual who, with his companion, beat up an old woman of seventy and stole her entire pension of two hundred thousand lire. The face of his accomplice will be shown later this evening, at 22.30 on Channel One."

CRITO Is there not a danger, O Socrates, that some criminals might be encouraged into further crime by the possibility of appearing on television?

SOCRATES That is certainly a risk, but if we want to improve humanity we have to presuppose an essential honesty lurking in the hearts of men.

CRITO Do you think that television can do more for the betterment of mankind than you yourself do by speaking to people face to face?

SOCRATES Perhaps. But we are always left with the problem that television cannot answer questions. It's like a man who talks non-stop and never listens to what anybody else is saying.

CRITO That's because its function is to inform, not to listen. One must always presume that after a broadcast spectators will then hold a discussion among themselves.

SOCRATES I've never known an Athenian family turn off the television in order to start a discussion. No, my friend, I really fear that our century is condemned to passivity! Women spend their lives watching television in silence, men go to watch football matches and take no part in any sport themselves, boys and girls dance alone without ever whispering sweet nothings to each other! Hear me, O Criton, speech is the real gift of God, dialogue the only alternative to conflict between enemies. Blessed are those who talk, even if they talk too much!